Medicine, Miracle, and Myth in the New Testament

Medicine, Miracle, and Myth in the New Testament

J. Keir Howard

RESOURCE *Publications* · Eugene, Oregon

MEDICINE, MIRACLE, AND MYTH IN THE NEW TESTAMENT

Copyright © 2010 J. Keir Howard. All rights reserved. Except for brief quotations in critical publications or reviews, no part of this book may be reproduced in any manner without prior written permission from the publisher. Write: Permissions, Wipf and Stock Publishers, 199 W. 8th Ave., Suite 3, Eugene, OR 97401.

Resource Publications
An imprint of Wipf and Stock Publishers
199 W. 8th Ave., Suite 3
Eugene, OR 97401

www.wipfandstock.com

ISBN 13: 978-1-60899-244-7

Manufactured in the U.S.A.

Contents

Preface vii

Acknowledgements ix

1 The Background 1
2 The Gospel Narratives: Mark's Tradition 13
3 The Other Gospel Traditions 44
3 The Acts of the Apostles 71
4 The New Testament Letters 88
5 Medical Metaphors and Allusions in the New Testament 103

Glossary 111

Bibliography 115

Scripture Index 117

Preface

THE AIM OF THIS book is to apply modern medical knowledge to the New Testament for the benefit of the general reader, although it is hoped that others, such as ministers and students, will also find it of use. How far it succeeds in its aim will be for the reader to judge. It should be said at the outset, however, that there is nothing anachronistic in such an endeavor. Human pathology, and the vast majority of diseases to which human beings are liable, have not changed significantly through the centuries. Cancers and infections were rife in biblical times, and the results of injuries have been the same throughout history. It has been the understanding of causation with associated improvements in prevention, diagnosis, and treatment that has changed. There is no real difference, therefore, in suggesting that a possible diagnosis for Paul's thorn in the flesh was post-traumatic epilepsy than it is to propose that the disease from which King George III suffered was porphyria. Paul's illness was viewed with suspicion by his contemporaries, the king was treated as a madman, but both today would have been offered effective therapy.

The attempt to apply developing medical knowledge to the New Testament is by no means a new endeavor, and it is one that will almost certainly have to be repeated as the boundaries of medical knowledge expand. Dr Richard Meade, court physician to King George II, appears to have been the first writer in English to attempt to provide a scholarly medical explanation for the diseases mentioned in the Bible in his book, *Medica Sacra*, published in 1749. Over a hundred years were to pass before a further attempt was undertaken, this time by the eminent Victorian physician Sir James Risdon Bennett in a work entitled, *The Diseases of the Bible*, published by the Religious Tract Society in London, and which went through three editions in the 1890s. It remained a standard reference text for many years and provided a coherent interpretation of the biblical data that was true to the limits of medical knowledge at the time. Other books have appeared since that time and there has been a marked growth of interest in the subject in the past few decades, although, unfortunately, much that has been written has come from the pens of those with little competence in medical science.

The apparent lack of any effective dialogue between biblical scholars and their medical counterparts continues to result in incorrect translations of medical terms, and a general absence of useful comment on matters of medical interpretation in the standard commentaries on the New Testament. There have been numerous studies relating to matters of medical interest in the Bible in medical journals and other publications over the years, but they are rarely referenced in theological publications, and biblical scholars generally seem to have adopted a condescending attitude to what are dismissively termed "medicocentric" interpretations. It is one of the odder phenomena of the academic world that while theologians and biblical scholars have gradually come to accept advances in some areas of scientific knowledge, they continue to be extremely hesitant about the application of medical science. One reason may well be that the application of medical science and modern diagnostic categories will run counter to many well-entrenched traditional beliefs and assumptions, although that could also be said of advances in knowledge in other areas. Certainly, some biblical scholars are on record as arguing that categories such as magic and spirit possession provide better contextual explanations of the work of Jesus for example, than do medical explanations, but this is to limit interpretation solely to the categories of first century thought and it can hardly be deemed satisfactory for the intellectual requirements of the twenty-first century. This study, therefore, seeks to bridge the current gaps for the general reader and to provide a coherent interpretation of the New Testament data that meets the criteria of modern medical science. Inevitably, advances in the understanding of the human mind and body will mean that much of what was once believed can no longer be supported, but this should not mean the destruction of faith. Rather, it should work towards a faith marked by integrity and honesty, and that remains ever open to intellectual enquiry and is not closed by dogmatic preconceptions. It is in this spirit of open enquiry that this book is offered to the reader.

J KEIR HOWARD
The Feast of the Epiphany 2010

Acknowledgements

MANY PEOPLE, KNOWINGLY AND unknowingly, have contributed to my thinking on the matters covered by this book over many years, and it would be an impossible task to mention them all. It is, however, a particular pleasure to record my indebtedness to my friends Professor Clyde Curry Smith of the University of Wisconsin, Professor Donald Capps of Princeton Theological Seminary, and Nerys Parry, a colleague and friend whose psychological expertise was invaluable in rehabilitating patients with chronic pain syndromes. I owe each of them a deep debt of gratitude for their encouragement, and without their often cogent comments and criticisms this study would be very much the poorer. I am also grateful to Christian Amondson, Assistant Managing Editor of Wipf and Stock, for his courtesy, help, and practical advice throughout the preparation of the final manuscript, and to John Mabon who has given much valued help with the task of proof reading. The patient support of my wife, Dorothy, throughout the long period of the book's gestation, has been essential to its completion and is beyond simple thanks. Finally, I gratefully acknowledge the permission of the University Press of America (a member of the Rowman and Littlefield Publishing Group) to utilize substantial portions of material which originally appeared in my more academic study, *Disease and Healing in the New Testament: An Analysis and Interpretation*, which was published in 2001.

1

The Background

THE CULTURAL WORLD OF the Mediterranean region and the Middle East in the period of the New Testament was one of remarkable complexity. There was a great profusion of ideas, both philosophical and religious, and medical practice reflected this welter of conflicting concepts, from the calm, sober, and rational approach of the best Greek physicians to the superstition and magic prevalent in the general populace. The practice of Greek and Roman medicine is discussed in considerable detail in all the major works on the history of medicine and there is no need for more than a brief introduction at this point in order to provide some background to this study of medical matters in the New Testament, allowing them to be set in the context of the life and thought of the world of the Roman Empire.

One of the first things that should be said about medicine in the ancient world is that there was an almost complete lack of any genuine understanding of the way in which the human body works. Knowledge of anatomy had grown over the years, especially of the skeleton and muscles, having been developed primarily by the Greek physicians and it was put to good practical use in surgery, particularly by the Romans. However, there was little understanding of the function of the internal organs, other than in the most general terms, and certainly no understanding of the physiological and biochemical processes that form the basis of life. Animal (and some human) dissection had uncovered much in the way of structure, but nothing of function, which was left entirely to speculation. Some argued, indeed, that dissection was useless anyway as it revealed only the structure of dead people, not the living, and there were also religious scruples against the practice. The heart provides a good example of the ancient knowledge of form without an understanding of function. It was recognized that it worked as a pump, but the great Roman physician

Galen, for example, thought that its function was to expel impurities on contraction and take in atmospheric air on expansion, in order to cool the body and generate the vital spirit necessary for life. Similarly, there was little understanding of human or animal generation and, although the structure of the female genitalia was known, the mother was generally considered as simply the recipient of male seed that grew within her.

Diseases in the ancient world were very largely defined on the basis of symptoms, something that will become very apparent when the healing stories in the Gospels and the book of Acts are considered later. As a result, conditions that were very different from one another tended to be lumped together simply because the presenting symptoms were the same. For example, the man described as suffering from "dropsy" in Luke's Gospel (Luke 14:1–6) was suffering from some sort of illness that was defined solely on the basis of fluid accumulation in the limbs or abdomen. This may have been due to any one of a number of causes such as congestive heart failure, kidney failure, or liver disease. Incidentally, the term "dropsy," found in English translations of the Bible, is thoroughly outmoded: together with other obsolete medical terms that should no longer be used in Bible translations. Because there was no proper understanding of disease, there was no rational basis for treatment, and medicine and magic were often impossible to separate, although the Greek physicians endeavored to maintain some sort of rational approach to their methods.

Nonetheless, in the course of many years of trial and error, experience had taught people that certain herbs would often alleviate symptoms of disease, and both Roman and Greek surgeons were often very skilful, particularly in dealing with the effects of trauma, such as broken bones and serious wounds. Much of this had come about as a result of treating wounded soldiers and it is a fact of history that many of the major improvements in trauma surgery have come about through battlefield experience. In New Testament times the basics of orthopedics were well known to the Roman and Greek surgeons and many of the operations performed used techniques and instruments that were surprisingly modern in design and undoubtedly highly effective. A surgeon's house was discovered and excavated at Pompeii some years ago and revealed over two hundred surgical instruments in use in the first century AD, many of which would not look out of place in a modern operating theatre. More recently, another surgeon's house in Rimini has been excavated, dating from the second century, and again remarkably modern-styled instruments were discovered. Wounds and surgical incisions were washed with wine which would certainly have reduced infection and, provided both this and surgical shock could be avoided, there were good surgical procedures for dealing with bladder stones, hemorrhoids, and even breast cancer (which seems to have been very common in Roman society), while cataract surgery was almost commonplace. The Roman physician Celsus (who will be discussed later) commenting on surgical treatment, remarked that its effects were more obvious than the medical treatment of disease, in which recovery might be the result of medications, a sound body or simply good luck! Perceptions seem not to change, as medical students used to remark of their mentors that surgeons knew nothing and did everything, whereas physicians knew everything and did nothing!

Magic, however, dies hard and amulets, charms, and other magical apparatus were used to protect against different diseases, as they were until relatively recent times. Indeed, even in this twenty-first century, there remain many in the western world who continue to adhere to understandings of disease and its treatment that can only be viewed as magical, such as healing crystals, iridology, and other fanciful approaches to the cure of illnesses, and the wearing of charms is commonplace. There are also many religious people in sophisticated western society who advocate healing practices that are little better than shamanism, believing in miraculous cures against all evidence to the contrary, and returning to a belief in demons or other "spiritual" entities as the cause of disease. Credulity is by no means confined to ancient or unsophisticated societies. Equally, however, it is important to recognize that not everyone in the days of the Roman Empire was credulous. There was a rational approach to disease as well as a magical one and this empirical understanding was at the heart of the great Greek medical tradition.

EMPIRICAL MEDICINE

The person whose name has been most strongly associated with the Greek medical tradition was Hippocrates. The approach to medicine with which his name has become associated was firmly empirical in its practice and generally rejected anything other than rational explanations for disease. It firmly rejected magic and popular superstition, and attempted to provide a reasoned basis for medical practice. Inevitably, however, it was prevented from carrying this approach forward due to the lack of any real understanding of the principles of normal body and disease processes. It was caught within the boundaries of knowledge that existed at the time and was further handicapped by never being able to free itself from the controlling influences of philosophical systems of thought. At the heart of Hippocratic thinking was the doctrine of the four "humors" and their related basic temperaments. Thus the person with a preponderance of "phlegm" would demonstrate a phlegmatic character, the one with over much "blood", a sanguine temperament, the one with too much "black bile" would be melancholic, and the one with too much "yellow bile" would be choleric. It had little if any value as a theory to explain disease, but a belief in the four humors persisted for centuries and, even to this day, the terms used for describing basic human temperaments have remained in normal parlance. From the standpoint of genuine science, however, the importance of these theories was that they were all open to empirical verification or, more importantly, falsification. They could thus be modified or discarded in the light of new knowledge, something which is not possible for magical and religious concepts whether they belong to the first or the twenty-first centuries. Greek medicine thus marked the beginning of a genuine secular medical tradition, divorced from religion, and free from priests and magicians. Nonetheless, it faced a significant problem in that there was no system for effective control of medical practice. There were several centers where medicine was taught and where there might be specialization in specific conditions, but although places such as Alexandria, Pergamum, and Laodicea attracted many students, there was no standard medical curriculum and no degrees or other recognized qualifications.

The ideas of the Hippocratic School had laid the foundation for what may be called a genuine scientific medicine, and others were to build upon it. The two great luminaries of the medical world in the period of the New Testament or immediately later were Celsus, who was a contemporary of Jesus, having been known to have worked in Rome between AD 14 and 37, and Galen, who lived a little later from about AD 130 to 200. Celsus produced a massive work that covered not only medicine and surgery, but aspects of philosophy, law, and agriculture. He was the first to record the four cardinal signs of inflammation, *calor, rubor, dolor, tumor* (heat, redness, pain, and swelling) that are still taught to every medical student two millennia later. He could hardly be called a physician, however, in the sense that he practiced medicine as a profession, although he treated his slaves (he had a slave hospital on his own estates) and members of his family with some of his remedies. Furthermore, he wrote for a wealthy readership and the same would be true of Galen a couple of generations later. Galen was a very different sort of person from the straightforward and pragmatic Celsus. He was argumentative and forceful, but was the first writer to demonstrate the importance of proper anatomical knowledge as the basis of all medical practice. Unfortunately, some of his anatomy was wrong as he transferred the results of animal dissection to the human body without any checks, and these errors were not to be corrected until the work of the great anatomists of the Renaissance period and later, particularly men such as Vesalius in the sixteenth century and John Hunter in the eighteenth.

These two giants, Celsus and Galen, span the period of the New Testament and undoubtedly represented the sort of thinking that formed the basis for the work of the best of Roman and Greek medical practitioners in the time of the early Church. From the days of Hippocrates, the standard approach of the physician was one of allowing nature to take its course. Good physicians did not interfere with nature and shunned any form of meddlesome intervention. They would have agreed with Voltaire's maxim to the effect that the art of medicine consists in amusing the patient while nature cures the disease. In one sense, they did not have a great deal of choice as the available effective therapeutic agents were few. The extract of the opium poppy was used to relieve pain, some of the essential oils such as peppermint, for example, could provide some relief in mild digestive disorders, and various herbs had been found to be useful in providing symptomatic relief in a number of illnesses, but many were of doubtful efficacy or had significant toxic effects. In addition, some astringents were available, myrrh being one of the more famous. Myrrh was also used for embalming, together with frankincense and aloes. These are mentioned in the New Testament and the embalming spices are recorded as having been used at the burial of Jesus. The lack of effective drugs did not prevent physicians from going in for polypharmacy, however, using a great number of ingredients to produce their own favorite remedies. The wealthy patient expected value for money and the more ingredients in the mixture the better it went down, especially with a little honey to help (rather than, as the song has it, "a spoonful of sugar," something not introduced into the Mediterranean region until about the seventh century

AD). The reality was, however, that the influence of the therapeutic agents available to the physician of New Testament times on the course of any disease was minimal to say the least and, indeed, this would remain the situation effectively until the nineteenth century.

Not all medical practitioners were of high quality, however, and there are many references in the inscriptions and writings of the time to fraudulent quacks and dishonest practitioners. Galen, himself, made caustic comments on those medical practitioners who did no more for their patients than to bleed them, put on a plaster, and give an enema. This was very much the pattern of treatment until well into the nineteenth century and there is a well known epigram celebrating the ministrations of the eighteenth century London physician Dr John Coakley Lettsom (1744–1813):

> When any sick to me apply,
> I physick, bleeds, and sweats 'em;
> If after that they choose to die,
> What's that to me, I Lettsom.

In reality he was a tireless and energetic physician, a man of genuine kindness and liberality, who was responsible for many medical innovations and benefactions.

However, to return to ancient medicine, there seemed to be a general feeling, shown in writers such as Plutarch and Cato, that at best, physicians were greedy and over-fond of public displays designed to attract patients, and at worst, were nothing but charlatans who murdered Romans. Moreover, physicians tended to be expensive and thus their treatment was a luxury affordable by only the more wealthy citizens, although frequently slaves benefited as their owners saw them as a valuable resource that needed to be looked after. Many of the wealthy estate owners built hospitals for the treatment of their large body of slaves. The other group within Roman society that had regular medical services was the army and the base legionary forts and barracks had well-constructed hospitals, particularly those away from large towns. Hospitals, however, were not part of the wider social services of the Roman Empire and would not become widespread until the Christian church began to provide such services attached to monasteries. That, however, was a development long after the period of the New Testament. In the Roman world, in general terms, it was only slaves and the military that had the benefit of hospital treatment for sickness or wounds. It is interesting that physicians do not seem to have been highly regarded in Jewish society, and they appear to have been classed as manual workers. There are remarkably few references to medical practitioners in the New Testament, other than in an occasional proverbial saying and the specific reference to Luke as a physician (Col 4:14), a gentile who was Paul's companion and possibly his personal physician.

FOLK MEDICINE

Folk medicine in its various forms was the way in which the great majority of the population received medical help. This was particularly the case for the poor, who formed the one large group of people who had little or no access to formal medical services. For them, medical treatment was primarily a matter of self-help, based on whatever local remedies may have existed, together with help from the traditional folk healers, from exorcists, and from the growing number of shrines dedicated to the god Asclepius, the Greek god of healing, although this was something that did not develop in a major way until the later part of the period spanned by the New Testament. The poor relied primarily on the help of the family or friends, but also consulted the itinerant or local healers who had developed a mixture of skills acquired over time, such as couching for cataracts, a wide variety of folk remedies, and particularly the use of magic with incantations, spells, and the use of amulets and charms to ward off sickness and evil spirits. The sort of "cures" that these practitioners recommended do not appear very different from those that were in general use in western society until relatively recent times and, in fact, continue to be used in some forms of "alternative" medicine. The Jewish Mishnah, for example, advocates a remarkable number of folk remedies, such as a silver coin for bunions, locusts' eggs for earache, honey for sores (which might have been useful), and vinegar for toothache. The Roman writer Pliny the Elder, who died in the eruption of Vesuvius that destroyed Pompeii and Herculaneum in AD 79, also collected various folk remedies from Roman society and these included the use of such strange and obnoxious materials as sow's dung, hyena's feet, snake skins, vulture feathers, and earthworms, made up in various unpleasant mixtures. Alongside these totally useless forms of treatment there were some herbal remedies that probably had genuine therapeutic properties. Many of the herbs used, such as dog's mercury, feverfew, vervain, marjoram, and wood sage remained in use for many years, and to this list may be added the various herbs and spices used in cooking, such as mint, rue, cumin, dill, cinnamon, and so forth, since culinary and medical uses were often not completely separated. Several of these spices and herbs are mentioned in the New Testament although in a culinary and not a medical context.

Those forms of illness that exhibited more bizarre symptoms, such as florid mental diseases, together with those that did not respond to the various remedies applied by family members or the local folk healer, tended to be put down to the influence of malign spiritual forces. Belief in demons was the rule and these could affect any aspect of human life, but in particular they were believed to be the agents of sickness. It has to be said that most of the evidence for magical practices and exorcisms comes from documents much later than the New Testament, such as the Greek Magical Papyri that date from the third century. The extent to which one can extrapolate from this material to conditions and practices in the time of Jesus and the apostles is a matter that is far from resolved. Whereas medicine attempted to base its practice on observation of the natural order of things and the disturbances of such order by disease, the practice of magic attempted to harness the unseen cosmic forces for its own ends. Exorcism must be seen as closely related to magical practices, although an exorcist need not necessarily be a magician. It should be noted, however, that Jesus was accused of being essentially a "black magician" because of the success of his exorcisms (Mark 3:22). Nonetheless, exorcism is a non-rational mode of treatment that depends on a world view that understands disease as being the result of malign forces that may be expelled from the sufferer by the use of suitable techniques. These techniques often utilized what are now called abreactive methods and these were among the methods used by Jesus, something that will be discussed later at the appropriate place.

In view of the importance of abreactive treatment methods, however, it is useful to make some comment on them at this early stage in the study. In situations of high emotional or other psychological stress, an individual may respond by avoiding the painful or difficult situation by developing one or more physical symptoms. There may be, for example, loss of speech, paralysis of one or more limbs, seizures or a wide variety of other apparently physical disorders. There is usually some degree of secondary gain as a result of developing these symptoms, for example, a Roman soldier who developed a paralysis of his right arm would be unable to fight, and similar responses to the fear of battle have been recorded frequently in modern times. These have variously been referred to as "shell shock" or "battle fatigue," and there seems little doubt that the vague, but debilitating ill health attributed to a variety of exposures in recent conflicts owes much to these psychological mechanisms. In the past these symptoms were referred to as "hysterical", but the current terms for such illness are dissociation and conversion disorders (that is the conversion of overwhelming stress into physical symptoms). It should be noted that this has nothing whatever to do with religious conversion.

One form of treatment that may produce a rapid, although often temporary, resolution of the symptoms of conversion disorders is called abreaction. The term means simply that the treatment results in a discharge of emotion and a consequent relief of symptoms. An emotional situation is induced that leads to the collapse of the patient followed by recovery with freedom from the symptoms. It is a method that is frequently used by religious healers who undertake their work in situations of high emotion and produce various forms of psychological break down, such as the phenomenon of "being slain in the Spirit" which is common in charismatic religious services, and in which there is usually total physical collapse followed by a sense of great well being. There seems little doubt that Jesus used similar techniques and these will be noted in the later discussions of the Gospel stories of his healings. They continue to be used in many forms of religious healing services today and may result in a marked improvement in psychological well-being, although this tends to be temporary unless there is regular reinforcement. Such methods, however, do not have any effect on mental disorders due to physical causes in the brain, such as schizophrenia and bipolar disease (manic-depressive illness) and indeed their use in such conditions may be very dangerous for the patient.[1]

DISEASES IN THE ANCIENT WORLD

A final question that needs to be addressed is what can be known of the illnesses from which people suffered in the time of the New Testament. What evidence there is comes from contemporary writings as well as a little from the New Testament itself, and also from studies of skeletons and

---

1. The whole subject has been extremely well discussed by William Sargant in his two books, *Battle for the Mind* and *The Mind Possessed*.

mummies from the period. Although accurate estimates are not possible, there is little doubt that life expectancy was low in the Roman Empire and was probably little more than twenty-five years at birth, with only about 8 per cent of the population living longer than sixty years. The poor life expectancy at birth was largely due to the very high infant mortality rates and it has been estimated that nearly 30 per cent of Roman infants had died before their first birthday. It is also certain that maternal mortality was also very high as a result of poor management of labor and related infections. Trauma and infection were almost certainly the main killers in the ancient world and two infections that were among the great scourges of Roman society were with little doubt, malaria and tuberculosis.

In spite of the excellent drainage systems and reasonably good water supplies of the major cities, the general levels of health in Roman society would be comparable to those of a modern Third World situation. This is not surprising as infections of all forms remained the major influence on the demography of most societies until the arrival of antibiotics in the mid-twentieth century. It is more than likely that the references to "fevers" in the New Testament are to malaria which was very common throughout the Mediterranean basin, but it is interesting that there is no clear mention of tuberculosis anywhere in the New Testament. One reason may be that, by its nature, it would not have been amenable to the healing methods of Jesus and his disciples, and was thus ignored as were other major physical diseases. However, there are probable references to tuberculosis in the Hebrew Bible as a wasting disease, for example at Lev 26:16 where it is mentioned with another disease that may well have been malaria. Other infections such as diphtheria, whooping cough, and middle ear disease, with its complication of mastoid infection, were described in the ancient texts and appear to have been common, and were probably responsible for much child mortality, although, once again, these common diseases fail to get a mention in the New Testament.

Epidemics of various forms were frequently noted in the ancient writings as well as in the Hebrew Bible, and would have been associated with the serious overcrowding in the cities, as well as during sieges in wartime. Among such epidemic diseases were bubonic plague, typhus, and typhoid fever, as well as smallpox, each of them well described in ancient literature. The New Testament references, however, are restricted to the book of Revelation and are no more than vague allusions to epidemics of high mortality which the writer believed to be the result of divine judgment. The role of parasites in transmitting disease was not understood and such infestations receive little mention in the Scriptures. There is, however, an interesting reference to what was probably scabies in the Hebrew Bible at Deut 28:27, and this would have remained a prevalent and uncomfortable infestation in New Testament times (as it continues to be today, although, fortunately, the condition can now be treated rapidly and effectively). Other parasites such as fleas, lice, and bed bugs, as well as ticks would also have been common, but again they are not mentioned in the New Testament, possibly because they were such a part of the normal experience of everyday life, although there are occasional references in the Hebrew Bible.

Cancers of different types were described in the Greek medical texts and breast cancer seems to have been particularly common in Roman society. Arthritis, osteoporosis, and osteomyelitis (chronic bone infection) have all been noted in many of the skeletons from ancient burials, together with evidence of severe dental disease, often affecting the jaw bone, indicating that life for the older people would have been in many cases miserable and painful. Skin diseases were also common and some mention should be made of leprosy. The biblical references to what has been translated "leprosy" in virtually all English translations of the Bible are generally agreed to have nothing to do with the specific disease called leprosy or Hansen's disease today. The biblical texts used the Hebrew word *sâraʿat* and the Greek word *lepra* to refer to a variety of skin conditions. The descriptions given are highly suggestive that these would have included psoriasis, seborrheic dermatitis, and fungal infections of the skin (as well as fungal infestations of buildings such as dry rot). By the time of the New Testament, however, it is likely that cases of true leprosy were being encountered in Palestine and elsewhere, the disease having possibly been brought into the area by soldiers returning from Alexander's campaigns in the East. The Greek physicians were certainly recognizing true leprosy by the first century and referred to it as *elephantiasis* (not the disease given this name today which is caused by a parasitic worm), a descriptive term that referred to the thickened skin and deformity seen in the lepromatous form of the disease. They did not use the word *lepra* for this condition. The consistent use of the Greek word *lepra* in the New Testament would indicate that true leprosy was not in view, but rather the sort of scaly skin diseases covered by the regulations in the Mosaic law codes of the Hebrew Bible. True leprosy was incurable until the twentieth century, but scaly skin conditions, such as psoriasis, often go into remission, thus allowing the sufferer to be declared "cleansed." [2]

This then was the Mediterranean world in the time of the New Testament. It was a world of contrasts. A world of the rational and the irrational, of medicine, folk healers and magic, and it would have to be said that, in this respect, it was a world not so very different from modern western society. Throughout the Roman Empire itinerant healers and exorcists moved about from town to town through the countryside, and into that sort of background Jesus and his disciples would have fitted easily. Jesus was not unique as a healer and exorcist, and his itinerant ministry would certainly not have been viewed as something out of the ordinary in first century Palestinian society. Equally, however, it was also a world in which St Luke would not have been in any sense out of place as a traveling physician attached to his patron's retinue, providing professional medical help as needed on the basis of the scientific principles of the time. It remains now to examine how the New Testament writers recorded and interpreted medical matters as they considered them to be relevant to their primary task of proclaiming the gospel. Most interest will understandably fall on the healing activity of Jesus as recorded in the Gospels, but other matters of medical interest appear elsewhere in the pages of the New Testament.

---

2. For a discussion of the nature of biblical leprosy see Browne, *Leprosy in the Bible*.

2

The Gospel Narratives: Mark's Tradition

THE MAJOR FOCUS OF medical interest in the Gospels lies in the stories of the healings and exorcisms undertaken by Jesus. The earliest collections of such stories would have been part of the oral tradition about the words and works of Jesus which was probably beginning to be collected even before the events of the first Easter. It also seems very likely that written collections were beginning to circulate among the small groups of Jesus' followers well before the middle of the first century. The earliest Gospel as such, however, is generally accepted as being the Gospel of Mark which was almost certainly compiled within thirty-five years of the death and resurrection of Jesus, and before the cataclysmic events of the Jewish War and the destruction of Jerusalem and the temple in AD 70. It was thus written at a time when first hand memory still existed and people would have been able to say, "I was there!" It is the height of folly to ignore the presence of personal memory in the Gospel narratives as it is in any modern narrative written within a few years of an event. The existence of such memories provided an important brake on over-fanciful developments in the early oral tradition, something that is sometimes forgotten.

The primary intention of the Evangelists was to present their understanding of the good news of God's action in Jesus. The stories about Jesus were thus stories to tell a story, but the fact that the primary function was evangelistic or didactic does not mean that the accounts of what Jesus said and did are not grounded in genuine memories of real events. It has become fashionable among some New Testament scholars to adopt a pose of extreme historical skepticism, but this often seems to be grounded in preconceptions rather than being based on genuine critical analysis of the data. The historian generally assumes that an author is trying to write history if that is what the written material appears to demonstrate. Not only so, but the historian will tend to trust the account unless there are clear reasons for not doing so. It will always be accepted that the accounts of history are reconstructions of events, for facts do not exist in a vacuum and are always subject to interpretation. There will probably be embroidery, bias, exaggeration, and evidence of vested interest, but stories that purport to tell history usually represent something that happened. The same criteria of critical historical analysis should be applied as much to the Gospels as to Caesar's *Gallic Wars* or other ancient histories.

This study, therefore, will take the accounts of the ministry of Jesus seriously. The Evangelists were creative writers who were concerned to interpret the words and works of Jesus for their contemporaries, nonetheless, there is a vividness about these stories, particularly in Mark's Gospel, that suggests that they provide an accurate reflection of those exciting events that had happened in Galilee within living memory, and that had been seen and remembered by a far wider circle than the immediate followers of Jesus. The Evangelists lived in what was very largely a verbal world and there would have been a welter of conflicting opinions and remembered stories circulating throughout Galilee. These circulating stories would have been the primary sources for those particular narratives that later came to be written down.[1] Stories certainly expand with constant telling, but the presence of members of the original group of disciples of Jesus (undoubtedly much larger than the inner group of the Twelve) in the various small post-Easter communities of what may be called at this stage "the Jesus sect" would have provided a significant check on the amount to which stories were embroidered and the tradition modified. It is contended that such a framework allows for a level of substantial historicity for the Gospel narratives in general and Mark's Gospel in particular, in spite of the editorial developments and the lack of a clear chronological framework.

The Synoptic Gospels (Mark, Matthew, and Luke) contain most of the material of major medical interest and they will be given the most attention. However, the Gospel of John, although demonstrating a much greater degree of theological reflection and interpretation than the Synoptic Gospels, should be accorded due weight as an independent historical witness to the ministry of Jesus. The amount of attention given by

---

1. The importance and accuracy of the oral tradition has been emphasised by J.D.G. Dunn. *A New Perspective on Jesus*, among others. Those of us who have lived in verbal societies know from experience how accurate oral traditions can be.

John to the healing activity of Jesus is very slight, but the stories that are recounted are of interest and will be given appropriate consideration.

This is not the place to enter into an extensive discussion of the sources behind the Gospels and their inter-relationships. Nonetheless, something needs to be said briefly about the so-called "Synoptic problem." There is general agreement that both Matthew and Luke have utilized Mark, or, as some scholars consider more likely, the same oral traditions that Mark used, in the production of their own volumes, as well as having access to another set of traditions (whether written or oral is still debated) usually referred to as "Q" (an abbreviation of the German word *quelle* meaning a source). This represents the material common to both Matthew and Luke, but not contained in Mark. It consists, very largely, of sayings of Jesus and is thus not of great interest from a medical point of view. There is one significant exception to this in the story of the healing of the centurion's servant (Matt 8:5–13//Luke 7:1–10), the only healing narrative in the Synoptic Gospels that also has a parallel in John's Gospel (John 4:46–54). In addition, the evangelists incorporated material into their Gospels that was derived from their own unique sources and these traditions also contain a number of stories of interest from a medical standpoint.

THE GOSPEL OF MARK

There is general, although not total, agreement that Mark was the first Gospel to be written. The evangelist set out to write a coherent narrative that turned the randomness of the isolated pieces of oral tradition into an ordered story. The oral tradition contained various stories related to Jesus' activities as healer and exorcist, and Mark has incorporated what were probably isolated units with no specific historical context into his narrative where he considered they best fitted. Nonetheless, these stories possess features that would indicate that they belong to an early stage of the developing tradition and most of them lack significant theological editing. They are, as one writer has put it, "untamed," and many of them seem to be close enough to the events themselves to retain the vividness of genuine memory, something that some New Testament scholars seem unwilling to recognize. The overall picture that Mark and the other Evangelists present of Jesus as healer and exorcist is essentially coherent and consistent, and it will be discussed in detail at a later point in this study.

The demon possessed man at Capernaum (Mark 1:21–28//Luke 4:31–37)

In view of the amount of interest in exorcism and so-called deliverance ministry in many contemporary church circles, it is remarkable how few accounts of exorcisms appear in the New Testament. There are, in fact, just six in the Synoptic Gospels and two in Acts. There are a few vague and generalized comments on the ministry of Jesus in the Gospels that mention exorcisms, but there is no sign of the excessive (almost pathological) interest in such phenomena that is to be seen in other documents from the early centuries of the Christian era, and that has resurfaced at various times in the history of the church, including modern times. The Evangelists are remarkably reticent about the specific effects of evil powers on human health. The people described in the Synoptic Gospels as being possessed by evil spirits were without exception suffering from illnesses that presented unusual and bizarre symptoms, such as personality changes or severe convulsions, and these set them apart from those suffering from the general run of common diseases in the community. With the limited understandings of what caused disease in those times, it is not surprising that the powers of evil were considered to be specifically responsible for illnesses that were associated with such strange and outlandish behaviors. The belief that evil spirits are responsible for diseases such as epilepsy and certain mental illnesses, such as schizophrenia, still exists in many societies, such as those in Central Africa where the author worked for a number of years.

A comparison of the two accounts of this event shows that Luke has expanded the story in various ways or was using a tradition in which the story was told in more detail than Mark's source. It seems possible, however, that Luke wished to emphasize the remarkable nature of the exorcism and the power that Jesus had over evil spirits. Both Mark and Luke emphasize the violent nature of the convulsions, and the picture presented is of a man suffering from a condition characterized by abnormal behavior and violent convulsions. The people of the town, not surprisingly, thought that he was possessed by an evil spirit. Jesus completely reversed the situation with a word of command in an atmosphere of heightened emotion, and stress, and in front of the synagogue congregation.

As in most of these stories, the details are relatively sparse, but the account strongly suggests that the man in the synagogue was suffering from what is called a dissociative reaction, an illness that used to be called hysterical neurosis. Such conditions were discussed briefly in chapter 1. It was noted that they often arise as a result of stressful events and were especially common in war time among soldiers over-exposed to battle conditions when it used to be called "shell shock" or "battle fatigue." The patient shows a set of signs and symptoms that closely mimic those of physical illness, but there is no evidence of any underlying physical disease that would account for these physical features. The essential quality of these conditions is the presence of symptoms and signs affecting neurological function that suggest the existence of a physical disease when, in fact, none is present. The patient thus "converts" the underlying mental stresses, which have become intolerable, into physical symptoms as a way of escape. Hence the condition is generally referred to as "conversion disorder," a name that has nothing to do with religious conversion. The range of symptoms that may be displayed in different patients is extremely wide and includes blindness, deafness, severe pain without an underlying cause, paralysis of various forms, bizarre gaits, and convulsions, often occurring dramatically in public, as happened in this story.

Jesus undertook the cure in a dramatic fashion. He appears to have used a method still employed frequently by faith healers and exorcists today. He pronounced a word of command in an atmosphere of excitement and raised emotion, following which the man went into a convulsive collapse. This sort of physical collapse often occurs in modern charismatic services and appears to be due to a temporary break down in the regulatory function of the brain stem. Following the collapse, the patient experiences a sudden mental and physical relief of symptoms. It has been a form of treatment known for centuries by various folk healers and such forms of mental catharsis were mentioned in Greek literature. Similar techniques have proved very valuable in war time conditions, for example after the Dunkirk evacuation in the Second World War, helping to get "shell shocked" soldiers back to battle. On the other hand, such techniques, although they may be helpful in the short term, are not usually effective in producing lasting results unless there is a program of supportive therapy. Without ongoing reinforcement, the cure is often short lived and the patient relapses with recurrent symptoms that may be worse than before. It seems very likely that there was an awareness of this in the parable of Luke 11:24–26.

Mark's emphasis is theological and he wished to draw attention, from the very outset of the ministry of Jesus, to his power and authority over the forces of evil. The sad aspect of the story is that although the evil spirits are pictured as recognizing who Jesus was, the response of the crowd was no more than amazement. It is the classic picture of the wrong response that occurs frequently in Mark, and points to the lack of discernment and understanding that was to dog Jesus throughout his ministry.

Simon Peter's mother-in-law (Mark 1:29–31//Matt 8:14–15// Luke 4:38–39)

This delightful little interlude seems to have been included in Mark's Gospel for purely personal reasons. It bears no theological significance, although this has not stopped some commentators from reading such interpretations into the story, as a glance at many standard commentaries will show. Luke, however, has tried to turn the story into an exorcism in line with his general tendency to expand any elements of power and wonder-working in the ministry of Jesus, although, it has to be said, that to understand evil spirits as the source of fevers would seem to have been in line with much popular thought at the time, as evidenced by the rabbinical writings of a slightly later date.

Details are minimal and the reader is told simply that Peter's mother-in-law was suffering from a fever of some kind. This is a word that describes a symptom rather than indicating any underlying cause. Any confident diagnosis on such a slim basis is impossible, but there is a reasonable possibility that the illness was malaria. In Roman times malaria was endemic throughout most of the Mediterranean basin and remained common in the Middle East until relatively recent times. In particular it was rife in the upper Jordan valley and the area around Lake Huleh and the northern shores of Lake Galilee until swamp draining operations were carried out early in the twentieth century allowing agricultural development to proceed. Greek physicians had, from very early times, recognized the different forms of the disease based on their observations of the intervals between attacks of fever. There is good evidence, in fact, that the Greek word for "fever" was used almost exclusively at this time to describe the rigors associated with what today would be recognized as an acute malarial attack. However, there was no notion of the underlying cause, except to note that these periodic fevers were associated with marshy areas. These provided the ideal breeding conditions for the anopheline mosquitoes that transmit the disease, although this causal connection remained unknown until the last decade of the nineteenth century when it was discovered by Sir Ronald Ross. It remains one of the most serious disease problems in the world.

Mark's story is so short on detail that it does not allow complete confidence in making a diagnosis as there are many causal organisms that are able to produce a fever, from bacteria to viruses as well as protozoa, as in the case of malaria. On the other hand, common things being common, there is good reason for thinking that Peter's mother-in-law was very likely suffering from an attack of malaria which had gone through the period of high temperature and rigors, leaving the patient in a state of lethargy and depression from which Jesus was able to rouse her sufficiently for her to get up and prepare a meal for her guests.

The sufferer from leprosy (Mark 1:40-45//Matt 8:1-4//Luke 5:12-16)

It is one of the unfortunate aspects of biblical translation that the Hebrew word *sâraʿat* in the Hebrew Bible and the Greek word *lepra* in the New Testament have been consistently translated by the word "leprosy" in virtually all English translations of the Bible, with the exception of the Good News Bible (Today's English Version). Some recent revisions of earlier translations, such as the New International Version, have at least incorporated a marginal note to indicate that the mention of "leprosy" in the text is not identical with the infectious disease known today as leprosy or Hansen's disease. It has to be said, however, that the apparent unwillingness to incorporate a more satisfactory term is really inexcusable as there is universal agreement that the descriptions in the Bible do not resemble modern leprosy in any way, knowledge that goes back at least to the nineteenth century.[2] Indeed, had the translators of the Hebrew Bible into the Greek Septuagint Version around 100 BC, and the writers of the New Testament a century and a half later considered that true leprosy was the disease in question, then it may be said with some degree of certainty that they would have been much more likely to have used the Greek word *elephantiasis*. This was the word used to describe true leprosy which was

---

2. The fact that modern leprosy (Hansen's disease) did not fit the biblical descriptions was demonstrated over 130 years ago. Dr W. A. Greenwood of Oxford, for example, noted ("Leprosy," 76–78) that the adoption of the term "leprosy" in Bible translation "was ill-chosen in the first instance, and has continued to confuse the whole subject down to the present time."

becoming known in the Mediterranean world in this period, possibly introduced initially from the east by Alexander's soldiers returning home from their campaigns or perhaps by itinerant traders.

True leprosy is a very specific disease caused by a bacterium related to the organism that causes tuberculosis. The organism primarily attacks the skin and the peripheral sensory nerves causing loss of sensation and this feature, which is the main characteristic of the disease, is not mentioned anywhere in the Bible. It seems very unlikely that such a specific and easily recognizable symptom would have gone unnoticed had the biblical disease been leprosy as it is known today. The paralysis and deformity, so often associated with the disease, are largely the result of secondary infection, as well as the result of trauma, especially burns, going unrecognized because of the lack of feeling in the hands or feet. The frequent facial disfigurement that occurs in some forms of leprosy (predominantly the lepromatous form) is the result of the skin and subcutaneous tissues becoming swollen and thickened. It should also be noted that the references in Leviticus and elsewhere indicate that what was called "leprosy" could also affect inanimate objects, such as the walls of houses or clothing, as well as people. The references in these cases are almost certainly to various forms of fungal growth such as dry rot and mildew.

The biblical descriptions of "leprosy," however, indicate that the primary sign was a scaly discoloration of the skin associated with what was described as "raw flesh," and "scales like snowflakes" (Lev 13, 14 and Exod 4:6, etc). Such descriptions do not fit any single condition, although they could fit a number of skin disorders, particularly psoriasis and severe seborrheic dermatitis, both of which are universally common disorders. There is no final consensus, and indeed, finality is probably impossible as the descriptions lack precision, and were probably intended to include what would now be considered as a number of discrete conditions, but which, in biblical times, were simply lumped together under a single descriptive term, and which made the sufferer ritually unclean. Psoriasis is certainly the disease that meets most of the descriptive features of biblical "leprosy."

Those who suffered from eruptive skin conditions of this type were described as "unclean" and were excluded from all aspects of the life of the community. Modern leprosy has also attracted similar opprobrium, and sufferers were regularly excluded from society in mediaeval and later times until relatively recently. Indeed, even today in some societies, sufferers from leprosy tend to be shunned and find it difficult to find employment. The fact that Jesus was not concerned about physical contact with such people was part of his welcome to those who were the outcasts of society for whatever reason. The diseases that Jesus healed were, almost entirely, diseases that cut people off from the worshipping community. His ministry was thus designed to show the open welcome for everyone to the kingdom of God, even for those previously excluded from the covenant community of Israel.

The fact that "leprosy" rendered a person "unclean" has produced a distinction from other illnesses in the Gospel narratives in the way the cure is described. "Leprosy" was "cleansed," rather than being healed. The sufferer was thus able to return to a normal life. In this story the sufferer entreated Jesus either to make him clean or to pronounce him clean. The Greek verb that is used (*katharizō*) may have either meaning and it is used in the Septuagint version of Leviticus to mean "declare clean" and this is almost certainly the meaning, in a different context, at Acts 10:15.

There is good reason for thinking that "to declare clean" is the meaning of the verb in this story and the original context was one in which an affected person came to Jesus as a recognized teacher to ask for a temporary certificate of cleansing. His plea to Jesus was thus, "If you are willing, you are able to pronounce me clean!" There is evidence that it was allowable for specially authorized teachers to inspect leprosy sufferers who lived away from the environs of Jerusalem, and thus could not get to see a priest at the temple, to provide a temporary certificate of cleansing having provisionally pronounced them to be clean. This would allow the sufferer to re-enter normal society again even though it would still be necessary to obtain a formal certificate eventually from a priest. Because of the reputation of Jesus as teacher, prophet, and healer, the leprosy sufferer approached him with a request to be pronounced ritually clean as his skin disease was in remission. Another Gospel story has Jesus being treated in a similar way when he was asked to mediate in a family dispute as would an appointed rabbi (Luke 12:13,14). Both stories provide an indication of the way in which Jesus was viewed by many of his contemporaries.

Jesus appears to have responded to the request with anger and indignation. The Greek texts of Mark are divided as to whether Jesus was "filled with anger" (*orgistheis*) or "filled with compassion" (*splanchnistheis*), and textual scholars are also divided as to which is the correct reading. The former reading, however, seems more likely, as it is easier to understand how a scribe might change the idea of anger to that of compassion rather than the reverse. Further, the reading of anger seems to fit the context much better and should be seen as the response of Jesus to a request that completely misunderstood the nature of his work. Jesus was not prepared to provide what was no better than a makeshift declaration and consequently he told the sufferer to go to the priests to fulfill the demands of the Torah. Mark's tradition, however, has passed this story on as an account of a cure of a disease and it is easy to see how such a misinterpretation of events could occur.

A diagnosis of psoriasis in this case would seem a strong possibility as spontaneous remissions are very much part of the pattern of the illness, something that would have been long recognized and which provided the basis for a sufferer to be pronounced ritually clean, and thus be able to return to normal society (an outcome that would have been impossible with true leprosy). Such a remission would fit particularly well with the man's request for a declaration from Jesus to confirm his cleansed status.

The paralyzed youngster (Mark 2:1–12//Matt 9:1–8//Luke 5:21–32)

Each of the three synoptic evangelists records this account of the healing of a paralyzed youngster ("child" in both Mark and Matthew, and only referred to as a "man" in Luke's account), although there are variations in the accounts that reflect their different theological interests and readership. Mark's account is straightforward and presents an authentic picture of the youth's friends breaking up the simple daub and wattle roof of a Palestinian village house and letting him down on his bed roll or pallet in front of Jesus. Luke has replaced this description with a much more sophisticated (and amusing) picture. The house has now been given a tiled roof and the man was let down on a couch, rather than a simple bed roll. While the scene would be more in keeping with Roman and Greek city life, one wonders what Luke's readers would have made of a story in which the man struggled away with a couch on his back after he had been cured, quite apart from the likely need for a block and tackle to let the couch down in the first place! Matthew also has the youngster of his story lying on a couch, but he makes no reference to the friends letting him down through the roof or of his taking his couch home with him afterwards.

The medical information is very limited. The fact that the lad was confined to being carried about on a pallet, suggests that he was paraplegic. However, the causes of paraplegia are many and varied, from the effects of trauma to infections and degenerative diseases. In the western world today, the commonest cause is trauma producing injury of the spinal cord. Such events are remembered and there is no suggestion of such a memory in this story (as there was, for example, in the story of Mephibosheth in the Hebrew Bible (2 Sam 4:4)). Various physical diagnoses have been suggested at different times by different writers, but it seems highly probable that, as in the case of the man considered possessed by an evil spirit at Capernaum, this is another example of a functional rather than organic disease, particularly as a paraplegia of true organic origin would not have been amenable to the form of treatment that Jesus used.

Partial or complete paralysis is a common manifestation of conversion disorders, and the level of attention provided by the four friends would be welcome to someone suffering from this type of psychosomatic disorder, providing additional support to the sufferer's belief that he was genuinely physically ill. Modern day patients often present to their physicians with symptoms and signs without any clear underlying pathology and they represent a frequent and ongoing challenge to the doctor's skills in diagnosis and management, perhaps especially the latter. In this case, the youngster appears to have suffered from a marked anxiety state associated with guilt feelings. This is a very common feature of this type of illness. It is very probable, in fact, that the young man saw his condition as the direct punishment for some real or imagined sin, and he was consequently overwhelmed by feelings of guilt.

The approach of Jesus in dealing with the youngster was to deal first with the cause of the underlying anxiety and pronounce his sins forgiven, thus removing the feelings of guilt. He was then able to move on to the cure of his physical symptoms by the same sort of approach that he had used with the man in the Capernaum synagogue. As in that case, the pronouncement of cure and the command to take up his pallet and go home was given in an atmosphere charged with heightened emotion and excitement. The authority displayed by Jesus, both in pronouncing the forgiveness of sins, thus removing the cause of the underlying anxiety, as well as in commanding him to get up and go home, was the key to the cure. It was the removal of anxiety in the assurance that his sins had been forgiven that enabled the young man to do what he would have found impossible a moment before.

The man with the "withered" hand (Mark 3:1–6//Matt 12:9–14// Luke 6:6–11)

This story may be styled a conflict story centered around the disputes between Jesus and the Pharisees on what constitutes work on the Sabbath day. The story of the cure is almost incidental and the real issue is whether it is lawful to do good and to cure on the Sabbath. As is so often the case in these Gospel stories, the details of the man's condition are very meager. Mark described him as having a "withered" hand. The verb that is used (*xerainō*) commonly means to dry up or parch and thus, by extension, to waste or wither. However, at Mark 9:18, the word has the meaning of being stiff or rigid and this is also a regular use for this verb. The man in the story may thus have been suffering from some form of paralysis of his hand or arm, or simply immobility caused by chronic pain, arising from such a condition as the shoulder-hand syndrome as a result of a frozen shoulder (adhesive capsulitis).

The condition of frozen shoulder is common and often has a spontaneous origin, although it may follow trauma. There is pain and immobility, and a marked restriction of shoulder movements in all directions. The condition is often associated with what is called shoulder-hand syndrome, in which the presence of an immobile shoulder is associated with a painful and swollen hand which is usually cold, and shows marked muscle wasting. The condition of frozen shoulder has been known for many years as one in which there is usually spontaneous recovery occurring over a variable time, quite frequently without the patient being aware that there has been any improvement. It is common for a patient to be seen by the doctor some time after the onset of the condition and show ongoing loss of mobility, although there is a full range of movement on examination. The patient had become so used to the loss of function that there was no awareness of recovery. The case of the man with the "withered" hand would certainly fit this clinical picture and it would provide a very plausible explanation of both the condition and the apparent cure.

An alternative, but perhaps slightly more likely, diagnosis would be that once again there is here a case of functional paralysis arising from a conversion disorder. Localized paralysis is common in these conditions.

This would be particularly true in a situation where there was secondary gain as in the case of a soldier being unable to use his right hand for his sword and thus escape the dangers of battle. A similar condition is quite common and is what is termed focal dystonia in which there is spasm and cramping of the hand muscles which become stiff and useless. The condition may occur in various so-called "occupational cramps" (there is a description of such a condition in the Old Testament at 2 Sam 23:10) and they are associated quite frequently with a degree of functional overlay. This type of pathology, with its predominant psychological component, is far more likely than a genuine neurological condition affecting the hand or arm, and it may reasonably be proposed that this man was presenting either with a psychosomatic form of illness, highly amenable to the type of treatment approach that Jesus used, or the spontaneous remission of a frozen shoulder that was probably associated with shoulder-hand syndrome.

The Gerasene demoniac (Mark 5:1–20//Matt 8:28–34//Luke 8:26–39)

This story has long presented problems for readers and interpreters alike. On the other hand, the very difficulties of the story, including the stampede of the pigs, may be considered as evidence of the substantial authenticity of Mark's tradition. The event took place in gentile territory, although the textual variants regarding the place name make it impossible to locate the site of the event with any certainty. The descriptions in Mark, however, suggest a site on the eastern shore of Lake Galilee and, geographically, the village of Gergesa (modern Kursi) would be the most likely setting for the story.

There is no need to examine the details of the exorcism closely. Suffice it to say that the details of the story have close parallels with the exorcism techniques used by the contemporaries of Jesus, and the method that he appears to have used would not have come across as markedly different to the onlookers from those of other exorcists of the time. The man himself suffered from a set of bizarre symptoms and unpredictably violent behavior that would have led inevitably to the conclusion that he was demon possessed. The local people left him well alone and had given up any attempts to restrain him. Much of his violence appears to have been inwardly directed with episodes of self-mutilation, and he suffered from a delusional state, believing himself to be one of the legion of demons that tormented him.

At first sight, the diagnosis appears to be relatively straightforward. The man exhibited grossly disorganized behavior, episodes of violence, and paranoid delusions in which he believed himself to be influenced by demons. Such features would suggest a florid paranoid schizophrenia. However, a very similar clinical picture may also exist in the manic phase of bi-polar disorder (what used to be called manic depressive illness) and acute mania may be very difficult to distinguish from acute schizophrenia, although the severe violence displayed by the patient in this story is rare. The similar features of these illnesses, in all probability, may be simply the final common pathway for many different conditions, and there are other diagnostic possibilities, although they are much less likely. However, the possibility that the man's condition was a psychiatric conversion disorder should not lightly be dismissed, in spite of the bizarre pattern of illness. The recovery in response to an authoritative command in an emotionally charged atmosphere would certainly point to this type of psychiatric illness as being the cause of the man's symptoms, rather than an illness caused by physical factors in the form of specific types of disordered brain chemistry, such as schizophrenia or bipolar disease in which a behavioral approach would have little effect. In this man's case, however, a behavioral approach to treatment, together with the psychological support given by Jesus, provided the important elements that were successful in obtaining a remission of symptoms in his conversion disorder, at the same time underlining the importance of a caring authoritative relationship as an essential part of successful treatment.

Several commentators have seen a socio-political context behind this story and seen in it a parable of liberation from Roman domination and oppression. The man at the center of the story was representative of the people oppressed by the legions of Rome and the episode of the pigs provided a symbolic satisfaction of the desire to drive the Romans like pigs into the sea. In this context it has to be remembered that pigs were an unclean animal for the Jews and they were (and are) forbidden to eat them. Equally, gentiles were unclean, and the Roman armies in particular were seen by many as desecrating the sacred soil of Israel. There is little doubt that there is an intention of acted symbolism in the story as the Evangelist has told it, but this does not necessarily negate the underlying essential historicity of the story about a man with a severe psychiatric illness being helped by Jesus.

The woman with the hemorrhage (Mark 5:25–34//Matt 9:20–22// Luke 8:43–48)

Jewish law categorized anyone with what could be classified as a discharge of whatever form as ritually unclean. For this reason a menstruating woman, as well as anyone who touched her, was regarded as unclean (Lev 15:25–27). Anyone with an ongoing discharge or a woman with menorrhagia, as apparently in this case, faced very considerable social disability and would have been treated essentially as an outcast. Jesus deliberately stepped outside the conventions and presented people with a message that in both word and action was essentially subversive to the accepted norms of Jewish society. His message emphasized that defilement was not something caught like a contagious disease, but like true holiness, arose from inner motives, attitudes, and relationships. The woman in this story had apparently been excluded from the community for some twelve years and would have lived in social isolation for all that time, cut off from normal relationships with friends and family. Her cure restored her to her true status as a daughter of the covenant. She was no longer an outcast, but had been brought home; the underlying message of all Mark's healing stories.

Mark makes an interesting comment on the ministrations of the physicians of the time (studiously avoided in Luke). The various forms of treatment advocated in the Roman period are well attested from contemporary records and were generally unpleasant, including vile concoctions to be taken, and strange actions to be performed by the sufferer. A rabbinic source, for example, recommended that seven holes should be dug in the ground in which branches from young vines should be burned. The woman was to sit by each one in turn with a cup of wine in her hand while the physician recited the formula, "rise from your bleeding." The fact that the woman in Mark's story grew worse, rather than getting better as a result of such therapy, is not surprising.

The word used in Mark and Luke to describe the hemorrhage is a general one used in contemporary medical texts for any severe bleeding. Matthew uses another verb for hemorrhaging in its only New Testament occurrence. Although none of the words is specific, there is little doubt that the woman was suffering from some sort of very severe and chronic uterine bleeding. The causes of such bleeding are many, although more serious forms of pathology, such as tumors, may be reasonably excluded in view of the chronic nature of the condition. However, apart from various physical causes, severe and excessive bleeding may arise from psychological factors. Anxiety, depression, grief, and so forth, may have profound effects on the brain centers that influence the menstrual cycle. Although an absence of menstrual bleeding is the more common result of such stress factors, excessive bleeding may also occur and is well documented.

It has been noted in previous stories that psychological factors seem to be prominent in the conditions that Jesus treated. The pattern of illness with which he dealt is one of primarily psychogenic disease, rather than physical illness arising from an anatomical pathology such as heart disease or cancer. In fact diseases of this latter type are conspicuous by their absence in the earliest strata of tradition. It is suggested that this woman's condition of dysfunctional uterine bleeding was essentially psychogenic in origin. Her condition was influenced by predominantly psychosocial factors and may, indeed, have been a conversion type illness. The increasing anxiety that her condition induced, together with the depression associated with her position as an outcast from society, and the effect of her illness in making everything and everybody she touched unclean, would have induced a vicious cycle in which her illness became self-perpetuating. It was not surprising that she approached Jesus in such a surreptitious manner.

The woman believed that Jesus possessed supernatural powers from God that could bring about a cure of her condition and Mark told the story in what are in effect magical terms with "power" flowing out of Jesus like an electric current. However, the fact that the woman probably perceived Jesus' power as in some way magical does not prevent a more rational explanation being given to the situation, any more than the local belief that patients in an African village have been affected by witchcraft prevents the visiting physician from treating them with modern therapeutic agents. In this case, the woman's inner conviction, coupled with the intense desire to be cured, as well as the obstacles in the way of gaining her desired goal, all provided the right sort of environment in which the necessary psychological release could take place, paving the way for the relief of her symptoms. The result was openly confirmed by Jesus in front of the crowd, an important aspect of "faith healing" of this type that has long been recognized as essential to complete the relief of symptoms. Although Mark has undoubtedly compressed the time scale with his favorite word, "immediately," it may be assumed that the woman certainly began to feel that her health had improved from the moment she touched Jesus.

The daughter of Jairus (Mark 5:21–24; 35–43//Matt 9:18–19; 23–26// Luke 8:41–42; 49–56)

This story forms the framework for the episode of the healing of the woman with the hemorrhage. That episode may have been included in its present place in order to provide a reason for the apparent delay in Jesus reaching the home of Jairus to deal with his daughter: the form critical aspects of the story are not important for this study. The story centers on the faith of Jairus, the president of the local synagogue, who implored Jesus to come to his home to cure his daughter who was suffering from a severe and life-threatening, although unspecified, illness. Mark stated that the girl was close to death and clearly she was not expected to recover. Matthew and Luke both go much further in order to emphasize the "miraculous" nature of Jesus' intervention and indicated that by the time that Jesus had arrived the girl was dead. Matthew, in fact, reported that the professional mourners were already at the house, making someone guilty of very precipitate action indeed with the father not yet returned.

The information provided by Mark is so limited that any genuine attempt at diagnosis can be no more than guesswork. It may be stated unequivocally, however, that Mark nowhere suggests that the girl was dead and that Jesus resuscitated her. Mark, representing the earliest written tradition of the words and deeds of Jesus, has no account of a dead person being brought to life by Jesus, unlike the later and more developed traditions of Matthew, Luke, and also John. Mark's story suggests an illness of recent onset and very rapid progress, leading to a comatose or semi-comatose state. In view of the very rapid cure (presuming that this was not an added detail) it seems extremely unlikely that a severe and acute infection, such as cerebral malaria or meningitis, was the cause of the little girl's condition. Various other conditions have been suggested, such as an unstable vascular system leading to lack of oxygen to the brain, but these are not particularly plausible. The effects of toxic agents also seem unlikely although not entirely impossible, and the possibility of a metabolic coma, such as may result from disturbances in blood sugar, carbon dioxide, or calcium levels should not entirely be discounted. Coma may also result from over-breathing with profound changes in blood chemistry, often occurring in panic attacks and other psychological conditions. However, the state of unconsciousness is usually of relatively short duration and thus unlikely to have met the criteria of this story.

Certain psychiatric states may mimic coma due to the varying levels of unconsciousness and lack of response that they may produce. In certain forms of psychosis the patient may display catatonia in which there is a complete lack of voluntary or responsive movements, and the patient lies in a stuperose state. Trance-like states may also exist in certain conversion disorders and it is not impossible that this was the situation in this case. Certainty is not possible, although some form of functional illness seems the most probable cause of the child's illness. The girl's age (given as twelve years), presuming this was correct, would put her in the pubertal age group in which functional disorders frequently tend to develop.

The Syrophoenician woman's daughter (Mark 7:24–30//Matt 15:21–28)

The outstanding feature of this episode is the uncharacteristically harsh words that Jesus apparently used to the gentile woman who came to him for help. The words have been described as "shockingly intolerant" and they would certainly appear to reflect what might be termed, Galilean xenophobia. It is interesting that no such intolerant attitude to foreigners is suggested in the story of the healing of the Gerasene demoniac, another gentile who was also living in a gentile area. The woman did not take offence, as might have been expected, but responded with wit and wisdom. Her comment about the "crumbs under the table" became incorporated into the beautiful prayer of humble access used in the service of Holy Communion of the 1662 Book of Common Prayer of the Church of England.

The sickness of the girl is almost incidental to the dialogue between Jesus and the Syrophoenician woman. It is not surprising, therefore, that there are no details about the nature of the girl's illness other than that she was "possessed by an unclean spirit." The story of the healing is simply a vehicle to hold the narrative in place, and it is the response of Jesus to the gentile woman, and her eventual blessing that is important. It is worth noting, however, that there is no indication in the story of any form of active exorcism. There are no commands to the demon, no suggestion of any direct action or intervention at all; the woman is simply told to go home as her daughter is now well. It is a reasonable presumption that the girl was suffering from some form of illness with unusual or violent signs and symptoms, in view of the statement about the unclean spirit. However, the simple reassurance that Jesus gave the mother in such circumstances, with no indication that he actually did anything other than provide reassurance, has led to an alternative, but interesting suggestion that it was the mother rather than the daughter who needed help.

Munchausen's syndrome is a well-known psychiatric disorder in which the patient simulates illness with what are often bizarrely exaggerated symptoms in order to gain attention or affection for themselves. This may lead to repeated surgical interventions or other forms of treatment, and patients will travel from doctor to doctor or hospital to hospital, producing fresh sets of symptoms, and demanding more and more treatment. It is a form of self-mutilation. Recently, interest has focused on women who show a vicarious form of this syndrome (Meadow's syndrome, or Munchausen's syndrome by proxy) in which they invent detailed symptoms and signs in their children in order to gain help for themselves, subjecting the child to unnecessary tests and procedures in the process. In these circumstances the child may often be injured or even killed. It is not impossible that this story reflects such a situation, although some may judge such a solution to the child's illness to be anachronistic. Unfortunately not enough is known about psychiatric illness in Roman times, but it is not entirely beyond the bounds of possibility that some such situation may well have existed and Jesus was able to provide the reassurance the mother needed for herself rather than her daughter. She thus went home to a situation in which all was well. In other words the possibility exists that the child had never been sick other than in her mother's mind. Such a solution to the story is highly speculative, but so is any reconstruction in a story so bereft of detail. It would, however, fit with the type of activity in which Jesus was normally involved, that is dealing with those types of condition in which the psychological aspects were predominant. The problem would be to fit such pathology into the context of the first century as psychological illnesses of this nature do not appear to have been recognized in the ancient world, although there is ample evidence from ancient medical texts and other writings that mental illness itself was a well-recognized phenomenon. However, the fact that it was the woman who went to Jesus alone, rather than taking her daughter with her to the healer, suggests that the girl may not have been ill, but in any case some sort of psychogenic problem may reasonably be assumed to have been at the heart of the problem.

The man with the speech defect (Mark 7:31–37)

From the medical point of view, the main interest in this story, about a deaf man with a speech defect, centers on the description that is given of the methods that Jesus used to accomplish this healing. Mark is the only Evangelist who provides this sort of detail and it suggests that it comes from an early and possibly eyewitness tradition. It would have been only later that details that may have been considered an embarrassment to the early church were edited out of the traditions as they became written down. Mark informed his readers that Jesus took the man aside, used saliva (a well attested therapeutic agent in the ancient world and used by Jesus on at least three occasions, here, at Mark 8:23, and John 9:6), touched the affected parts, sighed, and gave a command that has been retained in its Aramaic form.

It is not clear from the narrative whether the man was totally unable to speak or whether he simply had a speech defect that made it difficult for people to understand him. Mark uses an unusual word at v. 32 (*mogilalos*), occurring only here in the New Testament. It carried the meaning of speaking with difficulty or having an impediment in one's speech, and is so used by a number of Greek authors. It is used once in the Septuagint version of the Hebrew Bible at Isaiah 35:6 and in other ancient versions at Exodus 4:11, and Isaiah 56:10, although in these examples the meaning seems to be "mute." The fact that at v. 35, following the cure of his condition, he was said to be able to speak clearly would suggest that he was demonstrating some form of impediment to his speech rather than being totally dumb.

As previously noted, this story is one of the few accounts in the Gospels that provide some details about the methods that Jesus used to heal those who came to him with various illnesses. The use of saliva, touch, and physical manipulation, together with dramatic commands, would place Jesus squarely among the folk healers of his time. Further, the fact that these methods were recorded in the earliest traditions (although it would seem that the techniques became edited out of the accounts at a fairly early stage) would suggest that the earliest followers of Jesus did not see them as an embarrassment, and did not try to isolate him from his cultural milieu. The use of a command in this case would have been of little use had the man been genuinely deaf, and the dramatic methods used would suggest that once again Jesus was dealing with what may be termed a psychosomatic or psychogenic disorder. Deafness and mutism, or speech defects as in this case, are common features of those conditions described earlier as conversion disorders. The account of the therapeutic methods that Jesus used in this instance, although limited in the details, suggest once more that he was using abreactive techniques, designed to produce relief of symptoms in those suffering from what used to be termed hysterical illnesses.

The blind man of Bethsaida (Mark 8:22–26)

The account of the cure of the blind man at Bethsaida is unique among the Gospel narratives in providing the response of a blind person to the recovery of sight. It is also another account of a cure performed by Jesus in which the methods he used are detailed. Both these points are important as they provide the information on which a diagnosis may be made with some degree of confidence. Further, it is a story that bears all the hallmarks of a clearly remembered and detailed reminiscence of a very real event in the ministry of Jesus, in spite of the misplaced skepticism of some commentators.

Blindness was (and remains) very common throughout the Middle East. It is a condition capable of several definitions, and in this case perhaps the most important issue to decide is whether the man's blindness was congenital or acquired. Acquired blindness is the more common form and, apart from trauma, is usually due either to severe eye infections such as trachoma or measles, or as the result of cataracts. There are several reasons for considering that this man was suffering from acquired blindness, the most likely cause being severe cataracts.

The restoration of sight was recorded as taking place in two stages. Initially, Jesus applied saliva to the eyes (possibly for the very practical reason of removing dirt and dried secretions from the eyes before proceeding with the cure, rather than any supposed magical function) and placed his hands on them. He then asked the man whether he could see anything, a question that resulted in the rather enigmatic statement, "I can make out people; they are like trees, except that I can see them walking." It is very unlikely that this remark meant merely that everything still appeared blurred and indistinct, and that men and trees remained vague and shadowy objects, except that men walked and trees did not. There is no reason to compare men and trees at all in view of the size difference between them. Nor is it likely that the man confused the visual images of trees and men on regaining his sight, being initially unable to interpret what he was seeing, as is usually the case with a person who regains sight after being blind from birth and has not learned to interpret the new visual stimuli properly.

It is much more likely, in fact, that the man's statement arose from an initial visual confusion about the relative size of people and trees. As he regained his vision, there was confusion about size so that people appeared as big as trees. The medical condition that exactly meets this situation is the loss of the lens in the eye (aphakia). A very clear picture of what happened thus emerges, and the Gospel narrative may be seen to provide remarkably exact detail. It is highly probable that the blind man was suffering from severe and over-ripe cataracts, a very common condition in that part of the world. Jesus followed the standard practice of folk healers to deal with this condition by using manual couching. By placing pressure on the eyes as he "laid hands on him," Jesus caused the lens to fall back into the vitreous chamber of the eye. In cases of severe cataract such backward displacement of the lens occurs easily with minimal trauma. The practice of manual couching was continued in Europe until relatively recent times and is still used extensively in India, Pakistan and the Middle East. Villagers in Pakistan, for example, still wait expectantly for the arrival of "the eye man" to couch the cataracts of the many elderly people suffering from them.

The result of losing the lens from the eye's visual path is a distortion of size perception so that objects appear much larger. The loss of the lens also results in blurring of the images due to loss of focusing power. The end result would be exactly as the man described his experience in the story. In response to the query of Jesus, "Do you see anything?" the man replied by affirming that he was able to make out people walking around, but they look as big as trees! It is interesting (and a little depressing) to note that not one commentator on this passage to the author's knowledge seems to have grasped the real significance of the words and their appropriateness to the situation. It is reasonable to judge that these words represent eye witness testimony that became part of the oral tradition. Any theological symbolism that might be read into them is a very secondary consideration compared with the real life situation they reflect.

The story does not end here, however. Jesus again touched the man's eyes and Mark stated that he regained his vision completely and was able to see things clearly. This may be explained by an incomplete displacement of the lenses following the initial couching and such a good end result would have happened had the man been what is termed a "high myope." Such people tend to see much more sharply following cataract removal than normal people and traditional healers are often able to recognize those sufferers who will benefit most from their ministrations. Mark's tradition thus presents Jesus as acting as a traditional healer and it seems to be only the later arising traditions that have removed both the difficulties that Jesus encountered in his healings, as well as details of his techniques, almost certainly for apologetic reasons.

The boy with "epilepsy" (Mark 9:14–29//Matt 17:14–20//Luke 9:37–43)

The detailed descriptions of this healing in the Gospel accounts would all tend to point towards a diagnosis of major (grand mal) epilepsy as the condition from which the boy in the story was suffering. It is perhaps remarkable that epilepsy hardly features in the biblical records, as it is a relatively common condition in all societies and was noted frequently in the ancient medical texts. There is, in fact, no clear reference to epilepsy in the Hebrew Bible, other than the possible reference to "moonstroke" in Ps 121:6. It has been suggested that King Saul and the prophet Ezekiel may have suffered from epilepsy, but other pathologies provide a more adequate explanation of their abnormal behavior patterns. The only clear reference to epilepsy in the New Testament is Matthew's use of the rare verb "to be moonstruck" (*selēniazomai*). It is used of the boy who is the subject of this story (Matt 17:15) and again at Matt 4:24 in a more general context. The verb derives from the ancient belief that epilepsy was due to the influence of the moon. However, the great Greek physician Hippocrates, who wrote at length about this disease, considered that it was as much due to natural causes as any other disease. Nonetheless, the activity of evil spirits was often considered to be the cause of epilepsy as it still is in many unsophisticated societies.

Mark told his story in graphic detail with a detailed account of an actual attack occurring in front of Jesus. He also emphasized the abject failure of the disciples to do anything for the boy, as well as recording the corroborating evidence provided by the boy's father with regard to the long term nature of the illness. These features all suggest that a genuine recollection lay behind Mark's tradition. The boy's father had been greatly disturbed by the life-threatening accidents that had occurred, with the lad being in danger of burning in the fire or falling into water. These are just the sort of accidents that have been well-documented in major epilepsy and which often give rise to severe burns and other injuries. What is interesting about this account, however, is that although such accidents were reported by the father, they do not seem to have caused any significant injury and in real terms do not seem to have been genuinely life-threatening. Such a situation would have been most unusual in genuine epilepsy, a condition which accounts for a very high proportion of those children treated in hospitals as a result of burns, particularly in unsophisticated societies.

It is suggested, therefore, that epilepsy should not be assumed too readily to have been the diagnosis in this case. The different incidents that the father reported may well have been attention seeking activities on the part of the boy as he tried to draw attention to himself and his needs. It is not unreasonable, therefore, to consider that the boy may have been suffering from a conversion disorder of the type described earlier. It is not always easy, even for a modern physician, to distinguish between seizures due to a psychological illness and true epilepsy on clinical grounds alone, and without sophisticated tests, such as an electroencephalogram or brain scanning. It would have been virtually impossible in ancient times when there was no understanding of underlying pathologies and all forms of seizures were generally lumped together as being the result of demon possession, or something similar, in the popular mind.

In addition to the seizures, Mark also records that the boy was both deaf and dumb. Some commentators see this additional information as evidence of the conflation of two stories into one. The flow of the story, however, suggests a single event and a less complicated explanation seems more likely. The single pathology of a conversion disorder would explain all the symptoms. Indeed, the additional sensory disorders would point even more strongly to the existence of this type of psychiatric illness, one which would have been very amenable to the abreactive method of treatment used by Jesus.

Blind Bartimaeus (Mark 10:46–53//Matt 20:29–34//Luke 18:35–43)

This story seems to be very much an acted parable and has such a structured form that it might well have been constructed as a sermon illustration. The story has a primary focus on certain aspects of the Christian gospel, underlining what it means to follow Jesus. It has gone through such a considerable degree of editorial activity that it is now impossible to uncover any medical details; although it is reasonable to assume that the story retains the memory of a genuine event. It is thus impossible to provide anything approaching certainty about diagnosis. However, on the basis that common things are common, it is likely that Bartimaeus was suffering from advanced cataracts. The general impression from the healing narratives in the Gospels is that those who had their sight restored by Jesus were suffering from advanced cataracts that were treated by the practice of manual couching.

The death of Jesus (Mark 15:15–38//Matt 27:26–50//Luke 23:24–46// John 19:1–37)

There is universal agreement among the New Testament writers that Jesus met his death by crucifixion. Each of the four Gospels provides some details of the trial and execution, but, unlike certain forms of Christian piety and sentimentalism, they do not dwell on the details and make little mention of the degree of suffering that Jesus must have experienced. There are also significant differences between the accounts of the trial and execution of Jesus as recounted in each of the four Gospels that make it difficult, if not impossible, to harmonize them and produce a single coherent narrative that takes all these variations into account. From the medical point of view, however, these matters are not of major importance as the interest is limited to the actual cause of death which each account agrees was as the result of crucifixion. The Gospels, however, give no details and are laconic in the extreme, merely stating that Jesus was taken from the court to the place of execution and crucified.

Crucifixion was universally regarded with horror in the Roman world. It was considered a most cruel and disgusting penalty, called by Josephus, "the most pitiable of deaths," and Cicero referred to it as "the most cruel and atrocious of punishments." No one would mention it in polite society and it is surprising that the cross was so soon universally accepted as the symbol of Christianity (well before the end of the first century). The origins of crucifixion are uncertain, although there is a suggestion that it was first used as a means of execution by the Medes and Persians, who may have taken the idea from the Assyrian practice of impaling on stakes. From Persia the practice spread to the Hellenistic world in general as a result of Alexander the Great's conquests. It was the Romans, however, who seemed to have perfected the practice and made crucifixion the form of execution for the lower classes, such as slaves, as well as for political and religious agitators, pirates, and those who were deemed to be traitors to the state. It was an ignominious and barbaric form of execution that continued in practice up to the fourth century in the Roman Empire when it was eventually abolished by the Emperor Constantine. Usually, however, Roman citizens were spared this form of execution unless found guilty of high treason. In Palestine, Jews had been crucified in large numbers as the Romans took charge of the region and it seemed to become almost a matter of policy, with thousands of Jews being crucified during the Jewish War of AD 66 to 70. The record of Pilate's ten years in office in Judea includes some three thousand victims of crucifixion. Roman crucifixions were normally carried out by a specialized team of five called the *exactor mortis*. It consisted of four experienced soldiers, the *quaternion*, and a centurion who was in charge of the team. The Synoptic Gospels make reference to the centurion in charge of the crucifixion, but John alone mentions the team of soldiers (John 19:23).

The form of cross varied considerably and also the actual position of the body on the cross. The Gospels provide no real hint as to the type of cross on which Jesus was crucified, although the impression gained is that Jesus was upright and had his arms outstretched. Traditionally, the cross has been represented as being in the shape of an elongated plus sign, presumably based on the statement in Matthew that an inscription was placed above the head of Jesus, something that the other Gospels imply, but do not state specifically. The wording of the inscription makes it clear that Jesus was executed as a traitor and subversive. The Gospels also agree that a cross beam was used, and Jesus either carried this to the place of execution (according to John 19:17), or was relieved of this burden by Simon of Cyrene who was impressed by the Roman soldiers to undertake the task (Mark 15:21, Matt 27:32, Luke 23:26). The likely reason for impressing Simon of Cyrene would have been the collapsed state of Jesus following the lengthy abuse and flogging that he had received from the Roman soldiers.

The way the victim was hanged on the cross varied considerably as already noted, but it was usually either by being tied to the cross beam by the lower forearm or by being nailed. The implication of the Gospel narratives is that Jesus was nailed to the cross, although, perhaps surprisingly, only John is explicit about this in an account of a post-resurrection appearance of Jesus (John 20:27). The nails would have been driven through the lower part of the forearms between the two forearm bones (radius and ulna) in order to support the weight of the body. The Greek word for "hand" may also include the forearm, and it would certainly have been the case that the nail marks to which the Gospel of John alludes would have been in the lower part of the forearm, in the region that is usually (although not anatomically) called the wrist. Nails driven through the palm of the hand, which is the usual portrayal in religious art, would not have been able to support the weight of the body. Luke preserves the tradition that the feet of Jesus were also nailed to the cross (Luke 24:39–40). The discovery in Jerusalem in 1968 of the skeleton of a young man who had been crucified at a time roughly contemporaneous with Jesus provided evidence that nailing of the victim's feet to the cross was practiced. A single nail had been used, driven through both heel (tarsal) bones, probably with one foot over the other so that the legs were twisted or else with the heels nailed to the sides of the cross. However, there appears to be no evidence that the forearms were nailed to the cross in this case, suggesting that they were tied to the cross beam. This skeleton appears to be the only recorded case of a victim of crucifixion from Roman times.

Mark (15:23) records that someone offered the crucified Jesus wine mixed with myrrh (a resin obtained from various plant species of the genus Commiphora), presumably as a pain killer. Myrrh has mild antiseptic and astringent properties, as do many plant resins, and was included in western pharmacopoeias until relatively recently. However, it has no effectiveness as a pain killer and Mark seems to have been misinformed on this point. Jesus refused the offer, although there is another memory, preserved in all four Gospels, that Jesus was given a drink of sour wine at a later point in the crucifixion (Mark 15:36; Matt 27:48; Luke 23:36; John 19:29–30). Matthew (27:34) also suggests that Jesus was offered sour wine mixed with a bitter substance (the Greek word *cholē* may mean bile or simply something bitter, the latter being more likely). As is often the case in Matthew, this action seems to have been in order to provide a fulfillment of the Hebrew Scriptures, particularly Ps 69:22 and as a statement of literal fact it has to be treated with caution.

There has been much speculation about the exact cause of Jesus' death. A very extensive review of the available literature was undertaken by Maslen and Mitchell in 2006.[3] They noted at least ten differing theories and made the point that when "a large number of theories are proposed for a problem in any scientific discipline, this often demonstrates that there is no clear evidence indicating the answer." Further, care has to be taken that the narratives in the Gospels are not taken necessarily as literal factual statements. Perhaps more than at any other place in these stories, the accounts of the Passion were concerned to link what was happening with the ancient Hebrew Scriptures and see the events of the death of Jesus as fulfilling, either literally or in a symbolic fashion, various passages from those Scriptures. The problem with some of the theories as to the cause of the death of Jesus is that they are dependent upon a literal reading of passages that were very likely to have been intended to be symbolic, such as the soldier's spear thrust and the pouring out of "blood and water" (John 19:34). It has too often been assumed that things happened exactly as recorded, but it has already been noted that it is impossible to harmonize the differing accounts of the crucifixion in every detail. John's account of the soldier's spear thrust has been considered on many occasions, but without reaching a consensus or developing any satisfactory solution that accounts for it in every respect which is not surprising should John's statement be symbolic rather than literal. A similar comment might be made also about the agony in the garden of Gethsemane and Luke's description of Jesus sweating what appeared to be great drops of blood (Luke 22:43–44). The phenomenon of blood stained sweat has been reported in the past, but the reports are not recent and have not been satisfactorily verified. No recent reports exist to the knowledge of the author. There is, however, considerable doubt whether these verses belong to the original text of the Gospel and textual critics agree that they are almost certainly a scribal addition going back to the second century. Most modern English versions omit them and on this basis the problem will not be addressed further.

3. Maslen and Mitchell, "Medical theories," 185–188.

One suggestion about the cause of Jesus' death should be dismissed from the outset. An English physician, J.C. Stroud, in the mid-nineteenth century, proposed that Jesus had died literally of a broken heart. He suggested that the heart wall had ruptured as a result of the immense physical and emotional strain of the trial and crucifixion. Blood accumulated and clotted in the membranes surrounding the heart (pericardium) and this was released as blood and serum (the latter appearing like water) when the spear was thrust in the side of Jesus. This theory became immensely popular, was seized upon by preachers and commentators, and featured in certain sentimental hymns of the time. Remarkably, it is still put forward from time to time and has even appeared in some commentaries in relatively recent years. It is high time that the theory was quietly buried for good! Apart from anything else, rupture of the heart is extremely rare, other than as a result of a piercing wound, and it is always associated with severe heart disease together with evidence of chronic heart failure for a considerable period of time before the actual rupture occurs. It is not a condition that occurs spontaneously, nor as a result of emotional or other pressures. It is perhaps worth adding that this theory has nothing to do with the so-called "broken heart syndrome" which is heart failure as a result of the effect of high levels of adrenaline on the heart muscle that may occur in situations of high emotion or stress. Although death may occasionally occur in this syndrome, it is as a result of acute heart failure and not heart rupture. That high levels of adrenaline, as a result of the intense stress under which he had been placed, may have been a contributory factor in the death of Jesus, is, of course, not disputed.

The two most likely causes of death proposed in recent times have been either asphyxia or severe shock occasioned by loss of blood and dehydration (hypovolemic shock). However, studies have indicated that death by asphyxia would have been unlikely with the arms outstretched on the cross, and would probably have only occurred had the arms been held directly above the head, preventing respiratory movements. There is no suggestion that this was the mode of Jesus' crucifixion and it does not seem to have been a method in wide general use. On the other hand, severe shock would have been a very likely result of significant blood loss (to which the previous beatings by the Roman soldiers would have contributed, as well as generally weakening him), together with dehydration from the long period of three to six hours on the cross. In addition, it is most unlikely that Jesus would have had anything to drink throughout the lengthy trial and the walk to the place of execution and, as indicated earlier, the effects of extreme stress and emotional trauma would very likely have contributed to the development of a shock syndrome.

There is considerable evidence from contemporary records that death did not usually occur rapidly and it was not uncommon for victims of crucifixion to last for days, although they would have almost certainly been unconscious well before the end. This was clearly the thought behind John's reference (19:31–33) to the breaking of the legs of the victims by the soldiers to hasten death so that the bodies could be removed before the Sabbath. However, even here a theological motive is apparent, as he wished to emphasize that Jesus' legs were not broken in keeping with the statement of Exod 12:46 (and also Num 9:12) about the Passover lamb. The Gospel traditions, however, certainly preserve an awareness that Jesus died much earlier than expected, and it seems most probable that he died as a result of profound and irreversible shock, brought about by the loss of blood volume and disturbed electrolyte balance that were also associated with a final cardiac arrest. It is likely that the shock syndrome evolved gradually over a period of hours with progressive reduction in blood flow in the body, eventually leading to irreversible tissue damage. Both heart and brain activity would have been depressed to the point of ultimate cessation of function and death, and his death would have been hastened had there also been a final cardiac arrest as has been suggested. This would certainly account for the apparent rapidity of Jesus' death. The few seconds of premonition when he called out to "give up" his spirit, together with the sudden final collapse, certainly carry the hallmarks of a cardiac death. However, it needs to be emphasized that the foregoing reconstruction is no more than hypothetical; certainty about the cause of death is impossible with the limited data available.

The foregoing discussion is dependent entirely on the assumption that Jesus actually died on the cross. Several writers have argued that Jesus did not, in fact, die in this way. The difficulty in diagnosing death and, in particular, distinguishing between clinical death and genuine brain death has been noted in earlier discussion about cases of resuscitation. There was no way of making such distinctions in Roman times and comatose, and similar states were often mistaken for death. In 1991 Trevor Lloyd Davies and his wife[4] produced a carefully argued case for considering

---

4. Lloyd Davies, and Lloyd Davies. "Resurrection or resuscitation?" 167–170.

that Jesus was not dead when taken down from the cross, but rather was suffering from severe hypotension (low blood pressure) caused by the trauma he had suffered and being fixed in an upright position for some six hours. A person in this state would be unconscious and have an ashen white skin, with imperceptible pulse and respiration: in the world of the time he would have been considered dead. However, provided that the brain had sufficient blood supply to be able to continue functioning at a minimal level, then recovery could occur once the person was placed in a horizontal position and brain circulation was restored. The Lloyd Davies argument has also been put forward by others in varying forms and at different times, and while undoubtedly plausible, it fails to do justice not only to the universal conviction throughout the New Testament that Jesus had genuinely died on the cross, something that even his enemies appear to have accepted, but also to his having been apparently fit and active within three days of such an experience as crucifixion which is rather hard to accept. The existing evidence, therefore, is all in favor of Jesus being actually dead when taken down from the cross.

Christian testimony, however, has always maintained that Good Friday was not the end and that God raised Jesus from the dead. The New Testament writings clearly view this event as something very different from the mere resuscitation of a dead person. It was understood as a new creative act of God and thus it transcended all previous experience of God's activity in the world. Christians today hold widely differing understandings of the resurrection of Jesus, and ultimately the acceptance of the reality of this event is a matter of faith. As such it can only be discussed in religious language and is not something open to scientific analysis: it can neither be verified nor refuted. For this reason it will not be discussed further in a book dealing solely with verifiable situations.

3

The Other Gospel Traditions

THE GOSPEL OF MATTHEW

MATTHEW RECORDED THREE HEALING stories that are not found elsewhere in the canonical Gospel traditions. These are derived from his own independent source, probably from stories circulating in the oral traditions about Jesus extant at the time and in the place of his writing. In addition, he recorded the story of the healing of the centurion's servant, a story not found in the Markan tradition, but in both Luke and John. It has usually been assumed that this derives from the material designated as 'Q', but in view of the variants in the three accounts it seems more likely that it came from the circulating oral traditions used independently by the Evangelists. There are good grounds for considering that John preserves a more accurate tradition of the event and this particular narrative will be considered in relation to that Gospel. Matthew also recorded a tradition of the virginal conception of Jesus, as also did Luke, although the two accounts are very different in substance and clearly independent. Both accounts of this tradition will be discussed together in the section dealing with Luke's Gospel.

Who did Jesus cure? (Matt 4:23–25)

Among the various editorial summary statements about the ministry of Jesus, there is one of particular interest from the medical point of view. The statement is found at Matt 4:23–25 and it implies that the people Jesus cured belonged to clearly identifiable groups. Initially Matthew referred to "all who were in a bad way" (*pantas tous kakōs echontas*), but then he went on to narrow this down and described two particular groups of people. Firstly there were those who were in pain (*basanois sunechomenous*). This seems to suggest that he had in mind a group of people who had various illnesses, the main feature of which was continuous and severe pain (Matthew used a word that was frequently employed to describe the severe pains associated with childbirth). Today, it would seem very probable that these patients would be diagnosed as suffering from one of the various chronic pain syndromes. The interesting feature of such conditions is that the pain is often not related to any genuine underlying structural pathology. In some cases of chronic pain there has been an initial pathology, such as an injury, but although this may no longer be evident, having healed, the associated pain has continued long after the underlying cause has been rectified. Continuing chronic pain of this nature is now recognized as having a major psychogenic component and is treated with behavioral therapy in addition to the appropriate medicines.

The other group of people were classified as "demonized" and Matthew breaks this group down into two sub-groups: those who were "moonstruck" (that is, people suffering from epileptiform seizures) and those who were paralyzed. This group would have very much been made up of the sort of people whose illnesses would be classified today as conversion disorders, that is those conditions in which physical symptoms are present without a corresponding underlying physical pathology and which are due instead to the conversion of inner psychological conflict into an apparent physical illness.

Both these broad categories that Matthew listed would be recognized today as consisting primarily of psychogenic illnesses. Many of them would fall within the category of what Issy Pilowsky called, "abnormal illness behavior."[1] Such conditions have been observed throughout history and across all cultures, although cultural and religious factors have tended to determine how the conditions have been viewed and treated. The Evangelist's classification in these verses thus gives further weight to the view that Jesus dealt primarily with psychosomatic conditions that were amenable to the activities of a prophetic healer, the only other conditions being the small number of physical disorders that could be dealt with by the limited methods of the folk healer, such as manual couching to cure cataracts.

---

1. Pilowsky, *Abnormal Illness Behaviour*.

Two blind men (Matt 9:27–31)

This very short account of the restoration of sight to two blind men may well be a variant of the story recounted at Matthew 20:29–34, which is itself a variant of Mark's story of the healing of Bartimaeus. In both places Matthew has transformed the single blind man in Mark into two blind beggars and has altered the scene from the roadside to a house. Matthew's account is terse and compressed, allowing of little detail other than that Jesus touched the eyes of the blind men. This comment is likely to have been part of the original tradition, indicating the way in which Jesus restored the sight of blind people, giving further support to the view that he confined his activities to those suffering from advanced cataracts that would have been amenable to treatment by manual couching. It is suggested that this story also supplies further clues that indicate that Jesus worked as a traditional folk healer in the mould of a charismatic prophet.

The dumb demoniac (Matt 9:32–33)

This very short account is of interest in that it forms the basis of what appears to have been an ongoing controversy about the source of Jesus' power and authority (see also Mark 3:22–40, Matt 12:24, and Luke 11:15). There was a strong memory embedded in the early traditions that Jesus had been accused of what amounted to black magic in his healing ministry, and of being been in league with the demonic powers that provided his ability to work wonders. That such a controversy could arise would seem to indicate that there was nothing unique about the way in which Jesus cured the sick, nothing, in other words, that would have established his credentials without any question. People had to make up their own minds about him; there was no short cut to faith. For some, Jesus was a prophet, a man of God; for others he was a black magician in league with the Satan.

The man in this story was described as being both dumb and demonized. This latter term, as was noted with regard to the stories in Mark, was generally used of conditions marked by abnormal forms of behavior. It is likely therefore that the man was suffering from what is classified today as a dissociative illness in which his underlying psychiatric problem was being converted into physical symptoms that had no physical basis. It has emerged very strongly and consistently from the Gospel narratives that this was the predominant pattern of illness that was displayed by those who were helped by Jesus. Dumbness is well-known as a common manifestation of such disorders and thus this story would fit into the general pattern of the healing activity of Jesus that Mark had already set out in his Gospel.

The blind and dumb demoniac (Matt 12:22–23)

This story features in Matthew's Gospel simply as being the means of introducing the controversy about Jesus and Beelzebul, together with the strong statement about speaking against the Holy Spirit. Mathew narrated the exorcism with extreme brevity and the details allow of little in the way of medical analysis. It is possible that the story is a conflation of the two healings at Matthew 9:27–34 of the blind men and the dumb demoniac. In this instance it is almost as though this person's blindness was added as an afterthought and it was the lack of speech that was the important issue.

Once again, the description of the man who was cured presents features that would be consistent with a conversion disorder. Certainty is impossible, both in respect of the accuracy of the tradition here and the possible diagnosis. It may be said, however, that there is no reason why both functional (so-called "hysterical") blindness and lack of speech should not co-exist in this type of disorder, and both are well-documented features of conversion disorders. The restoration of sight and speech are said to have occurred in a confrontational situation, very much as the Evangelists have recorded in other situations where Jesus has dealt with this type of illness. Stories of this nature thus provide circumstantial evidence both for the methods that Jesus used in his ministry as well as the underlying historicity of the traditions.

THE GOSPEL OF LUKE

Luke has produced a Gospel that has marked differences from either Mark or Matthew. The Gospel is the work of an educated writer, well-versed in the methods of the historians of his time, and able to put together a coherent narrative. He claimed, indeed, to have written a connected narrative, attempting to set his story into its historical context with people, events, and times acting as his external points of reference. His concern was to set out a Christian view of history that saw the life and work of Jesus as the culmination of the ancient promises of God to his people, but he also saw that ministry being carried forward in an ongoing salvation history in the life of the church, and this was to form the emphasis of the book of Acts. There was a consistent emphasis on the power of God's Spirit throughout Luke's writings and this has certainly influenced his handling of the stories of Jesus' healing ministry collected from Mark's tradition as well as the source he used in common with Matthew (Q). His own material, however, derived from sources distinct from Mark or Q, accounts for nearly half the Gospel and it contains much of medical interest.

The frequent use of what has been judged to be accurate medical terminology by Luke convinced W.K. Hobart, in a much quoted work,[2] of the medical background of the writer of the third Gospel, who could thus be reasonably identified with Luke "the beloved physician." Later studies have indicated, however, that much of Luke's so-called "medical language" has parallels in the non-medical literature of the time and it thus probably shows no more than that the author of the Gospel was cultured, well-read, and well educated. On the other hand, it also needs to be pointed out that there are several examples of unusual words occurring in Luke and Acts, and nowhere else in the New Testament, which could be construed as indicating an author with more than a passing knowledge of medical terminology. It is not completely beyond the bounds of possibility that Luke the physician may have been responsible for an initial and early first draft, a "Proto-Luke," even though the final form of the Gospel comes from another hand and considerably later in time.

Zechariah's temporary loss of speech (Luke 1:18–23 and 59–65)

Luke began his Gospel with the story of Zechariah and his wife Elizabeth who were to become the parents of John the Baptist, in spite of their advanced age. The actual age of the pair is not indicated and all that may be genuinely assumed on the evidence is that Elizabeth was past the menopause, although Zechariah referred to himself as "old." Luke recounted a story that told how Zechariah learned, as a result of an angelic vision in the temple, that, against all the odds, he was soon to become a father.

In other words, Zechariah experienced a vivid and emotionally charged dream that, as is frequently the case, reflected an underlying psychological conflict, in this case the mental trauma of learning that he was

---

2. Hobart, *Medical Language of St Luke*.

soon to become a father. Following this intense emotional experience he became dumb. He was able both to read and write, but he was apparently also deaf, as Luke stated that the people had to make signs to him in order to communicate at the naming ceremony (v. 62). It is not impossible that, as an elderly man, he may well have been suffering from hearing loss to start with, and it does not feature prominently in the story. It is his loss of speech that was the main point of the narrative and nothing was said about any restoration of hearing, only the restoration of speech. Assuming that this story reflects a genuine event, the fact that the deafness appeared to have persisted after the restoration of speech would suggest that it was a genuine physical condition and not psychogenic in origin.

Sudden loss of speech may be the result of several medical conditions and a cerebral vascular accident (stroke) would not be unexpected in an elderly man, although it has to be said that the actual age of Zechariah is nowhere stated. On the other hand, everything about the story points to a psychogenic origin for the problem, particularly in view of its self-limiting nature and the fact that there was no related loss of power in arms or legs. The almost certain diagnosis is one of aphasia, or loss of speech, as a result of a conversion disorder, resulting from the emotional shock of learning that he was to become a father, together with the "flight from reality" in avoiding a confrontation with his wife and other people. As is not uncommon in such cases, function would be restored by a further emotionally charged event and this occurred at the naming ceremony for his baby son amid all the excitement of such an occasion. Loss of speech, arising suddenly after extreme emotion, lasting for a limited time only, and then just as suddenly cured, may be considered, with little doubt, to be a functional disorder.

Unusual birth narratives: (i) John the Baptist (Luke 1:7, 13, 18, 57–58)

The conception and birth of John the Baptist is recorded only in Luke and the account has to be seen as part of his composite picture of the unusual events surrounding the birth of Jesus. John the Baptist was an historical personage, independently attested by the Jewish historian, Josephus, among others. His later ministry was conducted in the Judean desert in close proximity to the region of Qumran and its ascetic community that gave the Dead Sea Scrolls to the world, and several scholars have suggested a link between John and that community. In view of his importance as the herald and forerunner of the Messiah, Luke has provided a tradition of an unusual and unexpected conception and birth of which the previously considered story about his father Zechariah forms a part.

There is little doubt that the tradition Luke received was heavily dependent on the Old Testament stories of similar conceptions in childless women, who were either past the menopause or else had hitherto been unable to conceive. The two classic examples were Abraham's wife Sarah and the conception of Isaac (Gen 18) and the prophet Samuel's mother, Hannah (1 Sam 1), and a comparison of these stories with Luke's account will show extremely close parallels between them, certainly too close to be accidental. It seems likely that either Luke, or the tradition he received, has reworked the story of John's conception into an event that was to parallel the miraculous conceptions of the great heroes of Israel's past, in other words the narrator has emphasized the theological importance of John the Baptist by the way he has told the story. This means that the details of the story need to be viewed with some degree of caution in respect of historicity.

The impression given by Luke is that both Zechariah and Elizabeth, John's parents, were elderly, although the phrase that they were "getting on in years" has an Old Testament background and may simply be to heighten the drama. It has to be said, however, that anyone over fifty would certainly be considered elderly, indeed old, in view of the short life expectancy of that time. The emphasis of the story is on Elizabeth who was now past the menopause, and had been unable to conceive throughout her marriage. This may have been due to any number of factors, physical or psychological, and it is impossible to hazard a sensible guess. However, pregnancies to post-menopausal women without the use of modern fertilization techniques are well documented (a woman in England conceived naturally with no form of medical intervention and had a healthy child at the age of 59 in 1997) and elderly men frequently father children. The birth of John the Baptist, as Luke told it, was undoubtedly unusual and out of the normal run of events, but there is certainly no requirement to consider it as in any way "miraculous," although it seems clear that for theological reasons, it was undoubtedly Luke's intention that it should be viewed in this way.

Unusual birth narratives: (ii) Jesus (Luke 1:26–38 and Matt 1:18–25)

It is Luke and Matthew who alone in the New Testament provide the tradition that the conception and birth of Jesus were other than normal. Without the birth narratives of these two Gospels there would be no indication anywhere else in the New Testament of a virginal conception. Neither Mark nor John have any birth or infancy narratives, and John in particular notes the general understanding among the contemporaries of Jesus that he was the normal son of Joseph the local builder (John 1:45; 6:42), although there are suggestions that people were aware that there was some sort of irregularity (possibly a hint of illegitimacy) associated with his birth (John 8:19, 41). There was a strong Jewish tradition, certainly by the second century, that Mary had been raped by a Roman soldier. A tradition of this shocking nature would be difficult to transmit directly and it has been argued (particularly by feminist theologians) that the possibility of illegitimacy becomes a sort of sub-text in the Gospels in an attempt to minimize the scandal. It has been argued that this explains the rather odd way in which Matthew's genealogy of Jesus was set out at the beginning of his Gospel with its emphasis on four women, Tamar, Ruth, Rahab, and Bathsheba, who were almost certainly gentile and of dubious morals. In using these examples, Matthew was directing his readers' attention to the reality of the divine care for these marginalized women in his genealogical lists. The emphasis of the birth stories was thus focused on an act of divine providence and care for a violated and humiliated young woman rather than on a poorly attested supernatural act of conception.

The New Testament letters, which are the earliest Christian documents to have been preserved, contain no hints that the conception and birth of Jesus was other than the normal result of sexual relations between a man and a woman. It is also certain that the proclamation of the good news by Paul and others was in no way dependent upon a doctrine of the virginity of Mary. Further, not one of the early confessional statements in the New Testament contains any hint of a virginal conception. This study is not concerned with a discussion of the theology that underlies the stories about the virginal birth of Jesus, nor the way in which church dogma has developed well beyond the given data, but solely with the medical implications of the stories. Nonetheless something has to be said about the possible backgrounds to the narratives in Luke and Matthew.

It seems very probable that the tradition of a virginal conception was confined to certain specific circles among the early Christians and it does not appear in Christian literature until relatively late. Matthew was aware of the tradition and used it as one of his examples of the way in which the life of Jesus literally fulfilled the ancient Scriptures, one of his favorite themes. He used the formula, "that the Scripture might be fulfilled," or something similar, on some ten occasions in the course of the Gospel. He used the tradition of a virginal conception in order to provide what he believed to be a literal fulfillment of the prophecy of Isa 7:14 (in its Greek translation in which the Hebrew ʿ*almah*, meaning a young woman, was translated by the Greek *parthenos*), although to use the passage in this way was to ignore totally its original historical context and meaning. Matthew was stretching meanings well beyond the intentions of the prophet. The Hebrew ʿ*almah* means simply "a young woman," and carries no connotation about virginity whatever. There was another Hebrew word which specifically meant "virgin" and which the prophet would have used if that had been what he meant to convey. Similarly, the Greek word *parthenos* was used simply to describe a girl or young woman who was as yet unmarried and again, not of necessity, a virgin in the strict sense. Mary's surprise and confusion may simply have resulted from the knowledge that, as she had not yet reached the age of puberty, she was not ready for motherhood, for the term "virgin," was used in Jewish parlance simply to designate a girl who was considered too physically immature to conceive. An early apocryphal Gospel (*The Protoevangelium of James*) supports a tradition that Mary was in her early teens when pregnant, although the canonical Gospels are silent on her exact age. The response of the angel in Luke's account seems to suggest that God could cause the pre-pubertal Mary to conceive in just the same way as he had caused the post-menopausal Elizabeth to become pregnant, since in Jewish parlance, a married woman past child-bearing age was considered a virgin for a second time. To be a little unkind to the evangelist, Matthew was out to score points by showing that the whole life of Jesus had been foretold in detail in the prophetic Scriptures. However, in some ancient Greek, Latin, and Syriac manuscripts of Matthew, the writer quite specifically asserts that Joseph was the father of Jesus: "Jacob begot Joseph, and Joseph, to whom the virgin Mary was betrothed, begot Jesus," although textual critics do not consider this reading to be original. As noted earlier, the Evangelists were concerned to underline the protection and status given to this girl who becomes, through God's action, the mother of Israel's Messiah, mirroring other such women in the Davidic line who received divine protection.

Luke also uses this tradition to emphasize the role of God's Spirit from the very beginning of the life of Jesus. There is for him a deliberate link back to the stories of Israel's heroes of the past, in which their birth was accompanied by signs of God's special activity, thus emphasizing that these were children of destiny and were to be vehicles of God's salvation for his people. Luke wished to emphasize that this Jesus was to be the vehicle of God's salvation in a new and unique manner that would include all people and not just the chosen few of Israel. His birth as son of God was the result of the action of God's Spirit and so too his followers become sons of God by a rebirth through the selfsame Spirit: as for Jesus, so also for his followers.

It has also been argued, although much less so in recent scholarship, that another possible factor in the development of this tradition was the need to identify Jesus as uniquely "son of God" for the purposes of the expanding gentile mission into the Roman world, in which divine parentage was a frequent claim for its heroes. Paul, writing about AD 56, quoted an early Christian affirmation of faith that described Jesus as "son of David" according to his natural birth, but shown to be "son of God," that is the divinely appointed king over his people, by the power of the Holy Spirit at his resurrection (Rom 1:3,4). In other words, it was the resurrection that identified Jesus as God's king. Mark, writing in the late 60s, however, pushed this affirmation back to the baptism of Jesus when the heavenly voice declared him to be God's "beloved son" (Mark 1:11). By the end of the century, however, both Matthew and Luke had pushed the origin of the divine sonship of Jesus back to his birth. The developing tradition thus produced a shift both in the time when Jesus was proclaimed to be son of God and also in regard to what the expression meant: the meaning shifted from being an affirmation of his status as God's anointed king to an idea of a divine personage.

From the medical point of view the question inevitably arises as to whether these stories may be taken at face value. The problems have been discussed frequently and in great depth, and do not need to be elaborated in great detail here. At the end of the day the issue becomes essentially a matter of personal belief coupled with one's attitude to Scripture, although the inclusion of Mary's virginity in the historic Christian creeds gives it a level of theological importance that is not to be found anywhere in the New Testament. It has to be said, however, that belief in the virginal conception raises immense biological questions in particular that make it difficult to accept at face value for anyone other than those who believe Scripture to be inerrant and infallible in every respect, and/or who adhere to church dogma unquestioningly. Even such a highly respected Roman Catholic scholar as R. E. Brown has commented that he had come "to the conclusion that the *scientifically controllable* (italics original) biblical evidence leaves the question of the historicity of the virginal conception unresolved."[3]

The most important of the difficulties inherent in the notion of a virginal conception is undoubtedly the genetic problem. Genetic material is carried from generation to generation by chromosomes in the nucleus of every living cell. Sex is determined in most animals, including humans, by the XY chromosome system in which two like chromosomes (XX) determine the female sex of offspring and two unlike (XY) determine the male sex of the offspring. An animal that carried only its mother's chromosomes (as would always be the case in virginal conception) would be female, since the Y-chromosome, the mark of maleness, is passed on solely through the father. In nature, where parthenogenesis (the development of offspring without male intervention) does sometimes occur, for example, in some invertebrates, lizards, and fish, the offspring are always female without exception in those animals that have the XY system of sexual differentiation. Although parthenogenesis has never been shown to occur naturally in mammals, mammalian embryos have been developed in the laboratory as a result of electrical stimulation of an ovum, or by other means, but again these have all been female without exception. It needs to be emphasized that without the normal complement of chromosomes, Jesus could not have been a properly human male. The existing records clearly affirm that he was, and the evidence is incontrovertible that he was a normal man in all respects, thus carrying the normal male Y-chromosome. There are other biological problems that arise from what is essentially a theological concept, but this is the most difficult to overcome for those who wish to accept the literal story of the virginal conception of Jesus as an article of faith: it is simply too difficult to assert the full "maleness" of Jesus if he had no biological human father.

3. Brown, *Birth of the Messiah*, 527.

There are also significant historical problems in the narratives, including issues that relate to the culture and life of the time. One important example relates to the likelihood that Joseph could have divorced his betrothed quietly and without any scandal in the way Matthew suggests. This would seem to have been impossible in the Jewish culture of the time, although it appears that there was more cultural freedom in ancient Galilee than in Judea. It seems best, therefore, to view these birth narratives as a retelling of the story in such a way as to embody and emphasize what were seen as important spiritual truths, especially to emphasize the fact that Jesus was uniquely empowered by God's Spirit in order to carry out his mission as the divinely appointed Messiah who was ordained to bring about God's kingdom. This sort of allegorical approach to historical narratives, in which there was a retelling of the story in order to emphasize spiritual truth, was common in Jewish religious literature at the time and was known as *haggadah*. It was an approach that would have been seen as perfectly acceptable to the first readers of the Gospels.

The widow's son of Nain (Luke 7:11–17)

This story and the story of the raising of Lazarus in John's Gospel are the only two unequivocal accounts of Jesus raising the dead, although each of the four Gospels makes reference to such an activity in a general way. It is perhaps of significance that Luke and John are generally regarded as the two latest of the canonical Gospels, probably separated by as much as fifty or more years from the time of Jesus' ministry. Admittedly, there is much scholarly argument about the date of the Gospels, but most scholars would give relatively late dates for both Luke and John. By the latter years of the first century there would have been very few eye-witnesses left to testify of what they had seen and heard, thus reducing the checks that eye-witnesses might have placed on the way in which narratives developed.

The close parallels between this story and the accounts of the Old Testament prophets Elijah and Elisha raising widow's sons at Zarephath and Shunem (1 Kgs 17:17–24 and 2 Kgs 4:18–37) would suggest that the narrative has been designed to fit with the old prophetic traditions, emphasizing the way in which the early Christians saw Jesus as the fulfillment of these traditions and the one in whom God was present and active by his Spirit as he had been with the prophets in times past. There is little doubt that the Elijah-Elisha cycle of stories in the Hebrew Bible form the matrix and model for the way in which much of the original oral traditions about Jesus were developed.

The clinical diagnosis of death is not always easy to make and would have been even less easy in ancient times. The normal practice in the Middle East of burying people within a very short time of being pronounced dead, a practice that persists to the present day, increased the chances of someone who was merely comatose being buried. Indeed, in spite of sophisticated medical practice in modern societies, people are declared dead from time to time at an accident scene or in a hospital ward, only to come round in the mortuary some time later to everyone's consternation. One such case involved an elderly woman who was possibly suffering from catalepsy. All vital signs appeared to be absent and she was declared dead, but revived in the mortuary some time later. In addition, many medical conditions may mimic death, especially catalepsy as already noted, and it seems probable that something of this nature was the situation in this story.

There are aspects of the story, particularly the site of the event in the obscure town of Nain, a town that archaeology has shown to have had walls and a gate as Luke noted, which would suggest that he was in touch with a genuine early tradition about the son of a local widow apparently being raised to life by Jesus. Luke's story would thus seem to reflect a real event in the life of Jesus. Nonetheless, it is reasonably certain that the story has been modified to meet the Evangelist's presuppositions and aims. It cannot be said unequivocally, therefore, that the young man was dead in the accepted sense of that word and certainly not in a manner that would satisfy the criteria of a modern physician or pathologist.

Little can be said about any underlying diagnosis as the data are simply not present. The most likely explanation is that the young man was suffering from some sort of temporary comatose condition or was suffering from catalepsy. The latter is a generic term for certain peculiar states often associated with a major psychosis (such as schizophrenia) in which the patient lies stiffly in a stupor (catatonia). Pulse and breathing are imperceptible and the patient has every appearance of being dead. It has been suggested that this was a probable diagnosis in this case, which is by no means unlikely as it is a condition that has frequently given rise to a misdiagnosis of death.

Road side first aid (Luke 10:29–37)

The parable of the Good Samaritan provides an interesting insight into the basic first aid that might have been practiced in everyday life at the time of Jesus. The story was told by Jesus as a response to the question, "Who is my neighbor?" Jesus described a man traveling on a road, well-known for its highway robbers, who was beaten up and robbed and left "half dead" (*hemithanēs*—an unusual word to be found in the writings of Galen and only here in the New Testament) by the side of the road (v. 30). He was eventually rescued by a Samaritan who applied some basic first aid before taking him to a local inn to recover (v. 34).

The treatment of wounds followed well-established and generally very effective procedures in the Greco-Roman world. In this story the approach consisted of bandaging the wounds after initially pouring on olive oil and wine. Terms such as "binding up" or "bandaging," and "pouring on" (of the oil and wine), as well as the word used for "wounds" (*trauma*) are used frequently in ancient medical literature, but are found nowhere else in the New Testament. It was such use of technical terms of this sort by Luke that caused Hobart to conclude that the writer of the Gospel was someone with a medical background and, by inference, Luke "the beloved physician." As noted earlier, the possibility that Luke himself was the author of an early version of the Gospel (a "proto-Luke"), possibly built round the pattern of the lives of Elijah and Elisha, should not be too readily discounted. The use of oil and wine for the treatment of wounds is well attested by the Greek medical writers. The emollient properties of olive oil were well known and wine would have acted as a mild antiseptic, assisting healing, although the mechanism of its action would have been unknown and its value simply a matter learned by trial and error.

The deformed woman (Luke 13:10–17)

The story of the healing of the deformed woman has often been interpreted as an exorcism and a number of English Bible translations seem to have made that assumption. The woman was stated to have had a "spirit of weakness," and this phrase seems to have occasioned difficulties for both translators and commentators alike. Several modern English translations have interpreted the phrase to mean demon possession, but such an interpretation is going well beyond the evidence. Nowhere in the Gospels does the word "spirit" by itself, without a qualifier such as "unclean," imply an evil spirit or demon and there is no suggestion of a demon being present anywhere in this passage. The phrase is much more likely to be a way of expressing the state of mind of the woman after so many years of suffering. Further, the additional phrase about being bound by Satan is again no more than a general statement designed to make the contrast with the bonds of animals that could be released on a Sabbath day to allow them to drink. The whole forms a fine example of the type of argument so beloved by the Rabbis: "if the one, then how much more, the other." The argument that Jesus used here may be stated simply: if animals may be released from their bonds on a Sabbath to allow them to drink, then how much more should this "daughter of Abraham," who has been bound by Satan for eighteen years, be released on a Sabbath. The statement has nothing to do with demon possession, but is simply a reflection of the general view that Satan was primarily responsible for all human sin and sickness. In Luke's theology, Jesus is the one who is bringing about the triumph of God's rule and the end of all bondage to evil.

The details of the woman's illness are limited. Luke merely noted that the woman was unable to stand fully or properly erect. It would appear that she retained some degree of spinal movement, but this was very limited. The expression "bent" is also unclear and may refer either to a sideways or to a forward curvature of the spine. Various suggestions have been made about the diagnosis including ankylosing spondylitis, tuberculosis of the spine, and osteoarthritis. Such conditions would certainly produce symptoms to meet the limited criteria provided, but structural lesions of this sort were not the type of disease that the Gospel traditions record Jesus as curing. As many writers have noted, there are simply no records in the early traditions of Jesus curing purely physical diseases or mending broken limbs or other specifically physical conditions. Another approach should, therefore, be considered.

The clinical picture presented by this woman fits that of adult scoliosis, a condition in which the patient is typically a woman in her twenties or thirties at the time of onset. The condition is often due to non-organic (psychosomatic) causes such as the conversion-type conditions that were very much the sort of problem generally dealt with by Jesus, as has been noted earlier. It may also be associated with chronic back pain, a condition itself that frequently occurs without any underlying evidence of pathology. In these cases, a functional curvature of the spine comes about as a result of the patient attempting to avoid muscle spasm, something that the author met frequently in his own specialist medical practice. It is very possible, therefore, that this woman's condition was essentially functional rather than being the result of anatomical pathology. This would certainly fit with the general pattern, seen in each of the Gospels, where Jesus dealt with conditions that were essentially psychosomatic in origin. Luke's comment that she straightened up immediately following Jesus' touch may be seen as a little piece of pious exaggeration. Recovery to normal function after eighteen years would take a little more time.

The man with "dropsy" (Luke 14:1–6)

The patient in this narrative is virtually incidental to the story itself which is a conflict story about what may or may not be done on the Sabbath. As soon as the man was cured, he disappeared home and took no further part in the proceedings. The story thus seems to have been told to provide a setting for a statement about the Sabbath, very similar to the one that Jesus made in the story of the deformed woman. It is impossible therefore to say anything definite about the "dropsy" from which the man was suffering. The Greek word used (*hudrōpikos*) is found only here in the New Testament and does not occur anywhere in the Greek version of the Hebrew Bible (the Septuagint). The word is not a diagnosis; it simply describes the result of some form of underlying pathology such as heart, kidney or liver disease in which fluid accumulates in various parts of the body. Today the term "dropsy" is outmoded, a term such as edema being used instead. It is surprising that modern versions of the Bible still persist in using outmoded medical expressions. Edema is a term used to describe the accumulation of fluid in the dependent parts of the body such as the ankles and legs, and it would be such obvious swelling that would have been particularly noted in ancient times. On the other hand, medieval physicians tended to use the term "dropsy" for the accumulation of fluid in the abdomen (ascites), and the Greek physicians would certainly have been aware of such a condition in their patients. The way in which Luke phrased the encounter would strongly suggest that Jesus could not have missed seeing the man which suggests that his condition was obvious to all.

The causes of fluid accumulation in the body are many, but the vagueness and imprecision of the term means that it is impossible to know accurately what sort of fluid retention was implied in this story, and it would be foolish to try and provide any diagnosis in this case. Not only so, but the story has probably undergone considerable modification in the tradition before it reached the evangelist. Consequently, it is likely that this episode constitutes the type of narrative that arose in the later developing traditions, when the cure of a wider range of diseases was being ascribed to Jesus than was the case in the earliest tradition. Heart or kidney diseases, with associated edema, are simply not the sort of conditions that Jesus was normally portrayed as curing.

The ten sufferers from "leprosy" (Luke 17:11–19)

This narrative is the only account of Jesus dealing with "leprosy," other than the account at Mark 1:40–45 and parallels. The problems of determining the nature of the biblical disease were discussed in relation to Mark's story. The story as set out by Luke is a beautiful narrative centered on the need to respond to grace with gratitude. The man who returned to thank Jesus for his action was not merely "unclean," but also an outsider, a Samaritan. He was thus doubly outside the community, but it was this outsider whose cleansing was transformed into salvation as a result of his response. The theology of the story undoubtedly has determined its final form as what might be termed a preaching narrative, ideally suited to didactic purposes. The narrative contains a number of features which would suggest that it is a composite tale, probably built up on the basis of the Markan story, and it witnesses to the way in which the oral traditions about Jesus remained unfixed and were still developing some four or five decades after the first Easter.

What was said about 'leprosy' in the consideration of Mark's account applies to this story. Further, should it be that this narrative represents a development of the tradition that Mark had used, then it follows that what was said both about diagnosis and the declaration of cleansing would also apply in this case. It may also indicate that there may have been just the one story in the original Jesus traditions involving him and a leprosy sufferer.

The high priest's servant's ear (Luke 22:49–51)

Each of the four Gospels records this event in the Garden of Gethsemane. Jesus was being betrayed by Judas and taken by the temple guards to be arraigned on charges of treason. In the middle of this confused and confusing scene, one of the disciples struck off the high priest's servant's ear with his sword. According to John's Gospel, the slave's name was Malchus and it was Peter who wielded the sword. It is only Luke, however, who recorded that Jesus restored the man's severed ear and one wonders how such an event occurring on that dreadful night could have been ignored by the other evangelists had it happened as Luke pictured it. The situation is easy enough to envisage. The disciple drew his sword and intended splitting the man's head open, but either because of inexperience with a sword, or the uncertain light with the dancing shadows caused by flickering torches among the trees, or perhaps because the servant partly dodged the blow, he succeeded only in slicing off the man's ear.

The ear has an excellent blood supply and had partial severing taken place, leaving the ear hanging down, but still with a pedicle of tissue holding it, it would have allowed for healing to take place provided the ear was replaced in its proper position. It may be presumed that the touch of Jesus was in fact to put the ear in place and one might further presume (or at least hope) that someone put a firm bandage over it which would allow effective healing to occur over the course of a few weeks.

THE GOSPEL OF JOHN

It is immediately apparent on reading the Gospel of John that the great interest in the healing activity of Jesus, so marked in the Synoptic Gospels, is almost entirely lacking. It has been estimated that accounts of healing amount to about five per cent of John's text, whereas in Mark, for example, they account for something like twenty per cent of the Gospel. The other feature of medical importance (and also theological, one might add) is the complete absence of exorcisms from the Gospel. The reader of John's Gospel would certainly not come away from it with a picture of Jesus as an itinerant wonder worker, or even as a charismatic prophetic healer in the tradition of Elijah or Elisha. Indeed, the actions of Jesus are never recorded as "wonders," but always as "signs." John has carefully selected the signs that he records for the spiritual symbolism they provide and not because of the content or effect of the action. The fact that he has chosen specific events to meet his purposes is likely to mean also that the stories have been molded to suit the purpose John had for them within the Gospel. Nonetheless, there is good reason to think that John was utilizing sources as ancient and as good as those of the Synoptic writers, even though the level of interpretation is far greater than in the Synoptic Gospels. John's Gospel needs to be treated seriously as an independent witness to the life of Jesus and given as much weight as the other Gospels. John records only four occasions on which Jesus provided healing, the final episode being the raising of Lazarus. The Gospel is thus of relatively limited interest from a strictly medical standpoint.

The nobleman's son (John 4:46–54//Matt 8:5–13//Luke 7:1–10)

This story is the only account of a healing performed by Jesus that occurs in both the Synoptic traditions and in John. There are several differences between the three accounts, thus providing multiple attestation for the event, and pointing to an historical core common to each version. John described the man who came to Jesus as a king's officer (*basilikos*), a term that was used to denote various royal officials, including officers in Herod's army. Matthew and Luke call him a centurion, and this probably also refers to an officer in Herod's army, which was modeled on the Roman pattern. It would appear from the accounts that he was a man of substance and status in the Capernaum community. The sick person was described as the official's son. John used three words to describe him. On one occasion he used *pais*, a word that is somewhat ambiguous and may mean either a servant or a boy; on a further occasion he used *paidios*, a diminutive, meaning a little boy, and four times he used the usual word for son (*huios*). Matthew used *pais* throughout his narrative and Luke combined this word with *doulos*, the normal word for a slave. It is possible, therefore, that the sick man was a personal servant of the official, what might be termed today an officer's batman. On the other hand, John has interpreted the word *pais* to mean the official's son, emphasizing this with the use of the diminutive as he pleaded with Jesus to come to his house before his little boy died, and it may be that this is the more accurate tradition.

The only medical information provided is that the son/servant was suffering from a fever. It was noted in relation to Peter's mother-in-law (Mark 1:30–31) that this term frequently meant a malarial fever and the chances that this was the case in this story are quite high. Both instances of febrile illness mentioned in the Gospels occurred in Capernaum, a low lying town on the northern shores of Lake Galilee and in an area that was marshy in those days. Malaria was common and those suffering a severe attack might well be close to death; they would certainly feel that way. In this case, John did not, in fact, record a cure taking place. He simply stated that the boy got better (the Greek has an aorist tense at this point to which English translations fail to do justice) and this would fit with a knowledge of the natural history of a malarial attack and an understanding that such attacks are frequently self-limiting. In effect, Jesus gave the official the assurance that the crisis was past, the fever had subsided, and the servant/son had now recovered and would live. Jesus, in fact, did nothing and the official had to believe that Jesus was right about the boy with no healing action taking place. He had to have faith that Jesus knew what he was talking about.

The sick man at the Pool of Bethesda (John 5:1–18)

The form of this story is very similar to the Synoptic accounts of healing. However, it should always be remembered that the form of a story says nothing about its historicity. If one were to read the clinical notes recording patient histories in any hospital, the forms would be similar, if not virtually identical. Thankfully, no one has suggested that it would be possible to judge the truth or otherwise of medical case presentation on the basis of the form in which it is presented. Historians tend to avoid this sort of trap, but New Testament scholars do not always see the hole in the road.

The story concerns a man who is said to have been unable to walk for thirty-eight years. He spent his time sitting by the Pool of Bethesda in Jerusalem (a name supported by evidence from the Dead Sea Scrolls), hoping to reach the water when it periodically bubbled up. A later scribe has added an explanatory note (v. 7), giving the popular explanation of why the water bubbled up. Nothing was said about the nature of the man's illness; he was simply described by John as having some form of weakness (*astheneia*). There is no clear suggestion in the narrative that he was paralyzed in the normal sense of the word, although it is clear that he was suffering from some form of condition that limited his movements. John indicated that he seemed to be able to get to and from the pool by himself, although apparently with difficulty and only slowly, and this is supported by the man's claim that he had no friends to help him. Indeed, what friends he may have had seem to have been happy to leave him alone to wallow in his misery. The main feature of his behavior throughout the story was a querulous grumbling that others can get to the healing waters before he can.

There are similarities between this story and that of the paralyzed man in Mark's Gospel (Mark 2:1–12). In both cases the underlying condition appears to have been some sort of functional loss of movement strongly associated with guilt feelings, although there would appear to have been marked contrasts in attitudes and behavior. The presence of guilt feelings seems to be made clear in the words of Jesus to the man following his relief from symptoms, "sin no more, in case something worse happens to you." Ongoing freedom from symptoms is dependent on reinforcement, particularly in someone whose inadequate behavior seemed unable to meet the demands of life. Jesus pointed the man to a way in which his mental health may be maintained in the future. There would have been many others at the pool with various forms of physical illness who were ignored by Jesus. As an experienced healer, he would have recognized the sort of person who would benefit from his ministry, and thus he singled out this man with his functional condition as someone who would benefit from a direct approach to the psychological basis of his condition, rather than those with essentially physical disorders. Although details are minimal, it would appear that Jesus once again used abreactive methods to accomplish the man's cure.

The man born blind (John 9:1–41)

This story is unique in that it is the only account in the Gospels in which Jesus is recorded as giving sight to a man with congenital blindness. It is worth making the point once again that there is no *prima facie* reason for doubting the reliability of the tradition that records the giving of sight to someone who had been born blind. It needs to be affirmed that there are many well-documented cases in medical history of those who were blind from birth gaining their sight. True, stories often gain additional features the longer they are told, and there can be no doubt that John's motive in recounting the event is theological. However, there are aspects of this story that reflect an underlying early tradition that retained an accurate picture of the methods that Jesus used in his cures that were frequently edited out of the traditions as they developed.

However, having said this, there are features about the story which suggest that an original tradition of a blind man having his sight restored has been developed by John for theological reasons into something more. The expression "from birth" is unusual, occurring only here in the New Testament. The normal Semitic expression would have been, "from his mother's womb" (as at Acts 3:2 and 14:8), suggesting that this statement about the congenital nature of the blindness may not have been part of the original tradition. In addition, the verb used for the recovery of sight in the story (*anablepein*) always means the restoration or regaining of sight: it is not a verb applicable to someone who had never seen before. It seems very likely, therefore, that the reference to being blind from birth was an addition to the story to emphasize the theological point that John was making.

Jesus was described as using saliva to make a mud paste, applying it to the man's eyes and then telling him to wash it off in the Pool of Siloam. There are clear and close similarities between this account and the story in Mark (8:22–26) of the man at Bethsaida in which saliva and manual pressure on the eyes are prominent features. The essential difference was in the use of mud, but again this seems to have been John's addition to the original tradition and it would seem very probable that, as in the story in Mark, so here also, the original story was of a man, suffering from severe cataracts, whose sight was restored by the traditional method of manual couching.

However, should the account in John represent a genuine memory of someone who had been blind from birth gaining sight, then the almost certain diagnosis still remains one of blindness from cataracts, although in this case they would have been congenital cataracts. Congenital cataracts of varying intensity most often occur as the result of a maternal infection during pregnancy transmitted to the unborn infant (the commonest by far being rubella or German measles) or else passed from the mother to the child at birth (such as gonorrhea). It could just have been an awareness of the effects of sexually transmitted diseases on the baby that gave rise to the question of the disciples about who had sinned to cause the blindness (v. 2), although it is more likely that this was simply an expression of the prevalent view that misfortunes were the result of individual sin. In this regard, the rabbis taught that ante-natal sin was a possibility, commenting that "when a pregnant woman worships in a heathen temple, the unborn child also commits idolatry." The disciples' question was thus not entirely academic in relation to the beliefs and culture of the time.

The cure appears to have been brought about in very much the same way as the restoration of sight to the man at Bethsaida, that is by the use of manual couching. This gives confidence that the underlying tradition is reliable, portraying Jesus as working as a prophetic healer. It would seem that Jesus regularly used the method of couching to effect the cure of cataracts and the only remarkable thing about this story is the apparent immediate ability of the man to recognize the objects he was seeing had he been blind from birth. Vision is a complex process requiring the brain to be able to interpret the images seen by the eye. This requires a learning process and it does not happen immediately. There are many examples of people who have been blind from birth who experience significant problems in being able to recognize what they are seeing after having their sight restored by surgery. Compression of time frames is not uncommon in the Gospel narratives, but it would certainly be most remarkable for a congenitally blind person to be able to recognize objects so quickly after the restoration of sight, as opposed simply to seeing them. It seems likely, therefore, that the man had some degree of partial vision before the cure.

It is rare for congenital cataracts to be so dense that they totally obscure vision, and the patient usually has the ability to make out larger objects at least, although they are seen through a fog. The man would thus have had some awareness of the nature and shape of things about him (taking the story at face value, for example, he seemed to have no problems in setting off for the Pool of Siloam and being able to find his way there unaided), and he would not have needed to learn the details of what he was seeing. On the other hand, he was probably left with problems of focus due to the lenses of the eyes having been pushed back out of the light pathway, as described earlier in discussing the story of the blind man of Bethsaida (Mark 8:22–26). On the whole, however, it would be more likely that the man in the story had severe, age-related cataracts, common things being common, and John has developed this original tradition of a story of the restoration of sight to a man with this common condition for his own theological purposes.

The raising of Lazarus (John 11:1–44)

The problems occasioned by this dramatic narrative are many. Quite apart from the central problem, particularly to modern minds, of the resuscitation of a man whose body had been decomposing in a tomb for four days, there is the major historical difficulty of fitting it into the life of Jesus. John recorded the event as a sign of unprecedented significance, a sign that was the final precipitating factor to bring the plot to kill Jesus to a head, yet none of the other Gospels has any mention of it. John has woven a brilliant literary creation, but in doing so he has effectively deprived the reader of any chance of discovering the nature of the event, what actually happened. It is possible that there is an underlying traditional story beneath the very complex construction that John has produced, and there have been numerous attempts to uncover this, without conspicuous success it has to be said. Nonetheless, the basic problems still remain for the modern reader, although John and his contemporaries did not have the least doubt that Jesus was able to raise the dead.

It is not improbable that the reference to the period of four days in the tomb may be additional to the original tradition and the core of the story may have been simply the raising of a man, considered dead by family and friends, along the lines of the raising of the widow's son in Luke's Gospel. The point about the length of time Lazarus had been dead had the function of emphasizing the remarkable nature of the event. Martha, in fact, was made to draw particular attention to this by her reference to the likely smell of putrefying flesh on opening the tomb, although there is no confirmation that this was the case as the story progresses. The restoration of someone not clinically dead, but either comatose or in a catatonic state, is likely to be behind this narrative, but it has undergone such major development that little more may be said about this event from the medical standpoint.

SOME GENERAL OBSERVATIONS ON JESUS AS A HEALER

It is worth making a few observations at this point, on the picture that emerges from the Gospels of Jesus as a healer. The Gospels describe the people who came to Jesus as being paralyzed, being deaf or dumb, being blind, and so forth. Such labels describe the presenting symptom or sign; for the symptom was the disease at a time when there was no understanding of pathological processes. Many different pathological conditions may show themselves with the same symptoms and signs, and for this reason it is often difficult to provide a diagnosis of those conditions mentioned in the Gospels that would satisfy modern diagnostic criteria. Nonetheless, there are sufficient clues that would indicate that the great majority of the conditions that Jesus dealt with were functional in nature.[4] That is to say, they were primarily psychosomatic disorders, rather than conditions with clear anatomical pathology. Illnesses of this nature remain common and would probably account for a high proportion of the case load seen by most family doctors in western countries. Many patients arrive at their family doctor with vague musculoskeletal and neurological symptoms together with problems of chronic pain, which come across as being very similar to those appearing in the Gospel stories. Psychosomatic disorders in general, and conversion disorders in particular, are common in all cultures, and in less sophisticated societies they are frequently put down to the influence of malign spirits as they were in the Gospel narratives.

A consistent pattern may be seen to emerge from the Gospels with regard to the healing work of Jesus. The types of conditions that he treated or helped seem to fall into the following three categories:

1. Firstly, there were those illnesses that may be described as psychosomatic in origin. It is likely that this definition would cover most of the conditions that were encountered and the great majority would fit into the classification of "conversion disorder," that is, conditions in which the complaints and symptoms are not the result of physical pathology, but rather are brought about by the transformation (conversion) of psychological conflicts into a range of often bizarre bodily symptoms. This group would include the various forms of paralysis, seizures, loss of speech, and so on that seemed to have been the presenting problems of most of the cases seen by Jesus. Jesus appears to have used psychological methods of treatment in his ministry and these were well known to traditional healers as a result of years of accumulated experience, both then and now. The meager details that have been preserved would suggest that his approach met the broad criteria that have been identified for the successful application of psychotherapeutic methods in cases of conversion disorders, particularly the use of behavioral therapy with abreactive techniques. Such a statement may appear

---

4. This study is not alone in reaching this conclusion. It was also reached independently by Capps, *The Village Psychiatrist*, as well as in earlier studies by Micklem, *Miracles* and Weatherhead, *Psychology, Religion and Healing*.

anachronistic, but it reflects the methods that traditional healers have used over many centuries.

2. The second group consists of diseases with genuine physical pathology, but which were amenable to the methods of treatment open to a folk healer. The best examples here are the blind people who went to Jesus and came away "cured." Few details have been preserved in the traditions, but the strong indications are that Jesus dealt mainly with the common problem of cataracts using the long established method of manual couching. Jesus also treated some patients with "fever." It was noted that this term very likely related to malarial fevers and his approach consisted essentially of reassurance, stemming from a knowledge of the natural history of a malarial attack. It may well be that Jesus "cured" other diseases within this category, but they were not remembered in the traditions that have come down through the Gospels: details may simply have become lost in transmission, or there was no obvious theological application, as there was with blindness, for example.

3. The third category relates to a set of specific conditions that have been labeled "leprosy" in most English translations, and which set the sufferer apart, and made him or her ritually unclean. As was discussed earlier, the term "leprosy" covers a group of skin conditions in which remissions would have occurred naturally. When the sufferer was free of symptoms he or she would have been able to be declared ritually clean and able to resume life in the community, rather than being declared as cured. It is not impossible that the tradition includes only one instance of Jesus dealing with this condition (the other accounts being variants of this one instance), and there is good reason to consider that what Jesus did was to declare the sufferer ritually clean as a result of a natural remission in the disease, rather than intervening to produce a cure. There is ongoing dispute about the interpretation of the story in Mark's Gospel and certainty is not possible. However, there are reasonable grounds for thinking that in this instance Jesus did no more than confirm to the sufferer that his skin problem had resolved or was at least in remission, allowing him to be officially declared clean and thus resume his place in society.

The Gospels thus present a coherent picture of Jesus working as a traditional healer and the picture is medically sound and convincing. His activity fell very much into the prophetic tradition exemplified by Elijah and Elisha in the Old Testament. It would seem that this was the way in which the populace viewed him, although his religious and political enemies were happy to accuse him of witchcraft and black magic. Others, however, were going about doing similar things, as the Gospels themselves note (Matt 12:27; Mark 9:38) and, although the later traditions such as Luke in particular, tend to expand and elaborate the stories, there is nothing about his methods that would set Jesus apart from other healers and exorcists of the time. A true understanding of Jesus came about through disclosure, that situation in which the penny drops and the ice cracks. Jesus is recorded as making just this point at Matt 16:17. The healing activity of Jesus is never presented as a proof of his deeper claims.

4

The Acts of the Apostles

THE BOOK OF ACTS forms a sequel to the Gospel of Luke and provides an account of the progress of the first thirty or so years of Christianity from the first Easter (around AD 28) to the arrival of the apostle Paul in Rome probably in the early part of AD 60. There will always be arguments about the dating of New Testament documents, but it seems reasonable to give a date of around AD 80 or possibly a little later for the Acts of the Apostles. It is a book of considerable medical interest as it records a number of apparent cures undertaken by the apostles (particularly Peter and Paul) which closely mirror those undertaken by Jesus in the Gospel narratives. There are also other occurrences of medical interest in the narrative.

Acts is one of the very few documents to give a genuine glimpse of the development of Christianity in its early years and is thus an almost unique document. There is no doubt that the author intended writing history. It has been remarked that he alone in the New Testament approaches the standards of the classical historians, standing in the line descending from Thucydides.

Nonetheless, there are problems in accepting Luke at face value, most notably his chronology, as well as the apologetic importance he gave to the miraculous element in the early apostolic ministry. It is certainly very likely that the apostles undertook healings and exorcisms in much the same way as had Jesus before them, but the question arises as to the extent that Luke has embellished his sources in order to give greater standing to the apostles in a world that placed considerable emphasis on wonders and "miraculous" events, a comment that is of equal relevance to his Gospel. He was apparently writing for a sophisticated audience, but nonetheless it would have been made up of people who accepted the reality of miraculous events, of magical powers, and the exorcism of evil spirits with a mixture of scepticism on the one hand and naïve credulity on the other. By the time that Luke was writing it would appear that the Christian church was already moving towards that attitude that saw the "miraculous" as an evangelistic tool, pointing to the power of the Christian God as superior to every rival claim.

The death of Judas (Acts 1:18–19)

The Gospel of Matthew (27:5) recorded the death of Judas Iscariot, the betrayer of Jesus, as a suicide by hanging. In Acts it is treated almost as a marginal note and he is described as having fallen, suffering severe and fatal abdominal injuries as a result. According to Acts he had bought a small farm with the blood money of the betrayal and the implication of this story is that he fell from the roof of the farm house. If he had fallen on to a stake in the ground or some other rough or jagged object and thus impaled himself, it would have been quite feasible for sufficient trauma to have occurred to allow his intestines to spill out of the wound. Such an injury would certainly have been fatal in those days (and probably also today for that matter). There is no way in which the account in Acts can be harmonised with the suicide of Matthew's story, in spite of the many attempts to do so, and the manner of Judas' death must remain in doubt.

There is, however, another ancient tradition that states that Judas swelled up and then burst open. This is based on reading the Greek word *prēnēs* in the text, as though it was connected with a verb meaning to swell up, rather than meaning lying prone on the ground. Several ancient versions provide this reading, and there was an early tradition that Judas swelled up and burst open, for which the early Christian apologist Papias was quoted as an authority. There is little doubt that this rather fanciful approach to the death of Judas was developed out of a desire to accommodate his fate to that considered appropriate to traitors and other undesirables, of which there are several examples in the ancient literature.

The gift of "tongues" (Acts 2:1–4)

According to Luke's account, the disciples of Jesus were together in Jerusalem immediately after the events of the first Easter when they experienced a remarkable phenomenon. It was as though each one of them had been touched with a flame and at the same time experienced a strong wind rushing through the place where they had gathered. They then began to speak "in tongues," a term that Luke must be using to mean different languages in this context, rather than being a reference to the ecstatic utterances mentioned by Paul in 1 Cor 12 and other places. Ecstatic speech of this nature is usually referred to as glossolalia and consists of a babble of noisy utterances rather than intelligible and coherent speech. It is a well recognised phenomenon and still occurs quite widely in both Christian and other religions, usually in situations of high emotional and religious fervour. Luke, however, almost certainly intended that his readers should understand that these disciples had spoken in foreign languages and he remarked that people were astonished that they heard what the apostles said in their own language. In other words, Luke emphasised that this was intelligible speech, not the meaningless gibberish of glossolalia. However, he seems to be true to his source when he recorded that some of the bystanders thought the disciples were drunk. This would suggest that some form of ecstatic and exaggerated behavioural display had occurred, for people in such a cosmopolitan place as Jerusalem at a major festival would be able to recognise different languages being spoken, as Luke clearly wished to suggest was the case. However, even had the bystanders not understood the disciples, they would hardly have thought of the speakers as drunk. Further, in Peter's speech that follows the event, it seems clear that some form of ecstatic experience was in mind as the event was seen as a fulfilment of Joel 2:28 with its references to dreams, visions, and prophecies.

There is little doubt that Luke's description owes much to Old Testament imagery and it carries major theological overtones. The appearance of wind and fire in the narrative is probably a deliberate link with Luke 3:16, and the ability to speak in different languages would seem to point to the universal mission of the church that is such a prominent aspect of Luke's theology. However, had the coming of the Holy Spirit been as Luke described it, then it is surprising that no reflection of the event occurs anywhere else in the New Testament, although there is a universal acceptance that the mark of the new Christian community is the ongoing presence of the risen Christ through his Spirit, providing it with its life, and giving it new direction and purpose.

The most likely explanation of the event, therefore, is that Luke has developed a memory of a group experience of ecstasy, occurring in the immediate aftermath of the events of the first Easter, to become the basis of his account of the giving of the Spirit. The events of that first Easter, in whatever way one may wish to interpret them, would have had a profound psychological effect on the first disciples. Gathered in a crowd, under extreme emotional pressure, it is not surprising that there was an experience of intense psychological release in the form of speaking with tongues, or "glossolalia." This phenomenon is mentioned elsewhere in Acts as well as in Paul's correspondence. As noted earlier, it is a well-documented response to high emotion that occurs today, generally, although by no means exclusively, in excitable religious services, and it occurs very widely throughout the world, and in most religions, Christian and non-Christian alike. It is essentially incoherent babble under extreme emotional pressure. Religious ecstasy may exhibit many forms including visions and trances, but the phenomenon of glossolalia is one of the commonest, almost certainly the best documented, and the most studied.

There are numerous other references to visions, dreams, and trance states in the book of Acts. To what extent these accounts are devices to underline the way in which Luke saw the prophecy of Joel being fulfilled is a moot point. One of the key points in Peter's speech at Pentecost was the fulfilment of the prophecy that God would pour out his Spirit and young men would see visions and old men dream dreams. Throughout the book there is a major emphasis on outpourings of the Spirit, similar to that of the original outpouring at Pentecost, an event that Luke does not seem to regard as being completely unique. He also records several visionary experiences and care should be taken, therefore, in interpreting every occasion as a literal description of an event. Nonetheless, there can be little doubt, particularly in view of other New Testament passages, that situations of intense emotion gave rise to various forms of mental phenomena, among which trances and visions would have been numbered. Some of these may also be seen as the resolution of inner conflicts, such as Peter's vision on the rooftop (Acts 10:9–16) in which the issue of gentile acceptance in the new community was resolved in his mind. Similarly, Paul's vision of the man from Macedonia (Acts 16:9–10) settled the direction he was to take in his future mission when he was undecided as to where he should go next. The subconscious mind resolved the problem in his sleep and provided a solution that the conscious mind may well not have accepted by rational argument.

The lame man at the temple gate (Acts 3:1–10)

This story follows on directly from the account of the remarkable happenings on the Day of Pentecost. It is told with that wealth of detail that is characteristic of Luke's story-telling, as well as with brilliant rhetoric, and the whole account, ending with the apostles' defence before the Sanhedrin, is an impressive literary construction. It is a story, however, that presents several difficulties, not least in regard to the cause of the man's lameness.

The man was described as being "lame from birth." There is no reason to doubt the tradition that Peter (was John an addition to the story by Luke?) healed a lame man in the temple precincts. The problem lies in accepting the statement that he had been "lame from birth," a comment that would suggest that he was suffering from some sort of congenital anomaly (club foot (talipes) being the most common), or possibly from the results of a birth injury. The severity of the condition was emphasised by Luke who indicated that the man had to be brought to his begging pitch by his friends and it is just possible that there is an echo here of the story of the paralysed man in the Gospels brought by his friends to Jesus. The cure itself was carried out by Peter in a manner strongly reminiscent of the way in which Jesus healed people. There was a crowd of people (it was at the hour of prayer) and in front of this crowd, Peter, on the authority of Jesus (the meaning of the expression "in the name of Jesus"), gave a word of command, "walk!" He then pulled the lame man to his feet.

The way in which Peter cured the man follows very much the pattern of abreactive therapy used by Jesus to deal with conversion disorders, as discussed in relation to the Gospel stories of healings. It is suggested, therefore, that the basic tradition of a lame man being cured has developed into a story about a man who was lame from birth. In this way Luke was intending to emphasise the extent of the power of God operating through the apostles. This tendency to extend the range of conditions that were healed to include long-standing chronic diseases is very much a part of the later traditions about Jesus and the apostles, and was no doubt a deliberate apologetic ploy to emphasise the triumph of God's power in seemingly impossible circumstances. It is suggested, therefore, that the original story was probably about a man with a conversion disorder affecting his legs and making him unable to walk. It thus forms a parallel to the type of psychosomatic conditions that Jesus cured in his ministry.

If this is so, then what the apostles were doing was not different in kind from what Jesus did in terms of traditional healing, and it may be presumed that they had learned the techniques during their time with him.

Ananias and Sapphira (Acts 5:1–11)

This is not the place to discuss the ethical implications of this story. It is clear that in its present position in the overall narrative, the account of the deaths of Ananias and Sapphira is to be put alongside the faithfulness of Barnabas in the previous paragraph. As it stands, the story retains a memory of the sudden death of two members of the early Christian community in Jerusalem. The husband and wife sold some of their property, but brought only a part of the proceeds to the apostles to be added to the common purse. Peter confronted each of the pair in turn, challenging their honesty. In turn, they both fell down and died when confronted by the authority and judgment of Peter, acting for all the apostles and in the name of God. As a result the whole church was struck with fear. There is little doubt that this fear is to be understood as a response to an abnormal and supernatural happening.

The story had probably become embroidered over the period before Luke set it down, but in societies that believe in supernatural powers being given to people, such as the shaman's power to bewitch, events of this type have been recorded. Sudden blindness, as will be met later (Acts 13:6–12), loss of speech and other manifestations may occur as conversion responses to extreme fear. Death, as a result of acute heart failure through stimulation of the sympathetic nervous system (cardiogenic shock), is an uncommon and extreme form of this type of reaction to intense emotional stress. It is not impossible, however, that neither Ananias nor his wife was actually dead. Indeed, it is possibly much more likely that the highly emotional confrontation with Peter in front of the congregation may have simply resulted in a profound faint (vaso-vagal syndrome) with loss of pulse, marked pallor, cold skin and other features that would resemble death. It has already been noted in respect of the stories in the Gospels, that death was not always easy to recognise and the extreme haste with which the bodies were removed in the story may well have resulted in two people being buried alive. However, the various features of the narrative may have simply accumulated with time as the story of two apparently inexplicable deaths in the community was told and retold. A similar overhasty judgment about death was recounted by Luke later in his narrative when Eutychus was thought to be dead after his fall, although fortunately Paul averted any precipitate action (see below on Acts 20:7–12).

Peter's shadow (Acts 5:12–16)

The remarks about people bringing out their sick in order that Peter's shadow might pass over them as he walked by is part of a summary statement about the miraculous powers of the apostles. Luke showed no reticence about adopting the popular view of miracles and his writings are characterised by a form of triumphalism in which wonders are an integral, indeed essential, part of the early Christian mission. At times he adopts a quasi-magical view of such wonderful events, and that certainly seems to be the case here. The approach to healing in this narrative would be labelled as superstition by many, and it is certainly reminiscent of the veneration of holy men and woman, and the attribution of miracles to them or their shrines, that is still to be found in some parts of the Christian church as well as in other non-Christian faiths. The belief that the shadow (or clothing, or remains) of a holy person is able to heal may provide a degree of benefit in some psychosomatic disorders and provide relief of symptoms which would then be interpreted as healing. This was very probably the situation that lay behind Luke's statements here, but that is a long way from seeing these incidents as "miraculous," and bringing about a cure of a genuine physical illness.

Paul's conversion and blindness (Acts 9:1–19//22:3–16//26:9–19)

Luke provides three separate accounts of Paul's conversion on the road to Damascus. The first of these forms part of his history, while the other two are set out as parts of speeches made by Paul at his defence, in one case before the crowd in the temple precincts in Jerusalem, and the other in a formal defence before Herod Agrippa. The accounts have minor variations that are probably to be accounted for by Luke's skilful story telling, but all mention the experience of seeing a brilliant light and subsequently suffering from temporary blindness. One of the problems with this story is that there is no independent confirmation of this experience in any of Paul's writings. There are extensive autobiographical passages, particularly in Galatians and 2 Corinthians, but nowhere is there any indication of the dramatic and awe-inspiring meeting with the risen Christ that Luke details in Acts. It is necessary, therefore, to treat Luke's story with some degree of caution, although there are elements in the narrative that point to an underlying authentic tradition. The most notable of these are the exposure to blinding light, the short-term blindness that followed, and the interesting description of the recovery of sight.

The accounts all agree that the blindness from which Paul suffered was directly associated with the blinding light. As he travelled to Damascus he was suddenly exposed to a brilliant light ("brighter than the mid-day sun" according to Acts 26:13). In the two versions of the story in which Paul was making his defence, it is recorded that his companions also experienced the same bright light. Everyone fell to the ground and following this exposure, Paul became blind. The whole is a good description of lightning stroke injury in which high intensity light causes flash blindness with varying degrees of retinal damage, usually, although not always, temporary, together with corneal burns. The amount of retinal damage would depend on the intensity of the light and the duration of exposure, and it may well have been the corneal damage that was more important in inducing the blindness. High intensity light is associated with heat, and this probably caused heat burns to the cornea. The cornea would have become opaque as a result of the tissue damage and the associated retinal effects would have together produced temporary blindness. Three days later, Paul's vision returned, according to Luke as the result of the ministrations of a local Christian called Ananias. The description sounds remarkably like the spontaneous sloughing of the damaged corneal cells and Luke has a throw-away remark that "something like scales fell off." It is interesting that the significance of this remark seems to have been missed in most commentaries on this passage, but it would be difficult to give a better description of the sloughing away of the dead cells covering the cornea.

It is possible that Paul's experience on the Damascus road may have resulted in some degree of permanent retinal damage, as well as contributing to the delayed development of cataracts. The immediate cause of blindness, however, was most likely lightning stroke injury with associated corneal burns. This experience became transmuted into a theophany, although Paul says nothing explicit about it in his own writings, other than claiming that the risen Christ had appeared to him.

The paralysed man at Lydda (Acts 9:33–35)

This appears to be one of two traditional healing stories about Peter (the other is the story of Tabitha at Joppa that follows) that Luke has incorporated into his narrative at this point. It concerns the cure of a man who had been paralysed and bed-ridden for some eight years. Luke's tradition has given him the thoroughly Greek name of Aeneas and, with little further elaboration, he was informed that Jesus Christ was about to cure him, and was given the command to get up and make his bed. The account is very similar to the stories of healings in the Gospels and it is possible that it may represent the re-telling of a story from those traditions that has become attached to a "Life of Peter." If one accepts the genuineness of the tradition, however, then it is a narrative that provides further evidence that the apostles utilised the same sort of methods as did their Master. Assuming that the story rests on a reliable tradition, then it is most likely that Aeneas was suffering from a conversion disorder. Some eight years previously he had been faced with some form of intolerable situation and the only response he was able to make was a flight from reality to being paralyzed: not a true neurological paralysis, but rather one that was psychosomatic in its basis. His cure follows the same psychotherapeutic methods used for similar conditions in the New Testament narratives and well-known to folk practitioners down the years. No more needs to be said about this event from the medical standpoint.

The raising of Tabitha (Acts 9:36–43)

The similarities between this story and the healing of the daughter of Jairus in the Gospels are so close, especially as it is presented in Mark, that some degree of conflation between the two accounts has almost certainly taken place, or it may be that a Gospel healing has been attributed to Peter. Miracle stories generally follow the same form, but this usually means no more than that they follow a conventional pattern of telling, just as folk tales frequently begin with the well-established formula, "once upon a time." In this case, however, the similarities are so close that it would seem that the same story has been told in two contexts.[1] It is very probable that the traditions about Peter's activities contained a memory that he had raised someone from the dead, but it is now impossible to untangle the

---

1. The two stories are set out in parallel to demonstrate the close similarities in Howard, *Disease and Healing*. 207.

exact circumstances and medical details. The inherent problems of narratives concerning the resuscitation of apparently dead people have been discussed earlier in regard to the widow's son at Nain (Luke 7:11–17) and the raising of Lazarus (John 11:1–44). The reservations expressed with regard to those accounts apply equally, if not more so, in this context.

The death of Herod (Acts 12:20–23)

Luke seems to show a certain morbid relish in detailing the occasion of Herod Agrippa's death. The account is in substantial agreement with that of Josephus, although the differences are sufficient to indicate that there is no mutual dependence. Both describe the occasion when Herod gave an oration to a large crowd and divine status was ascribed to him by the people. According to Josephus, he was immediately seized with violent internal pain, having seen an evil omen of an owl perched above him, and he died five days later. Luke also described him as being struck down suddenly (in this case, by God's angel), but his death was attributed to being "eaten by worms." The literal nature of this remark may probably be discounted, as it was a frequent description in ancient times of the way evil doers met their ends and was simply an attempt to give an unpleasant death to those who richly deserved it. However, both Luke and Josephus agree on the suddenness of Herod's death, and if Josephus is right in stating that he was seized with violent pains, he may well have died from a myocardial infarction (heart attack) or an acute intestinal obstruction which would have been almost certainly fatal. It should be said therefore, in defence of Luke, that acute intestinal obstructions may be caused by a heavy infestation of round worms which would have been evident in the faeces. There is insufficient evidence, however, to provide more than a guess as to the actual cause of Herod's death.

The blindness of Elymas (Acts 13:6–12)

The importance of this story from Luke's point of view is to show the contrast between magic and the revelation of God's power through Paul. The Jewish magician (his name is given as either Bar Jesus or Elymas) appears to have been attached in some way, possibly as a semi-official fortune teller, to the court of the Roman proconsul Sergius Paulus. He is represented as an enemy of the gospel and Paul attacked him with hard-hitting language, condemning him to temporary blindness.

There is nothing intrinsically improbable about this story, although some commentators seem to have problems with it, and it describes a form of conversion response to the commands of an authority figure. The writer has seen similar examples of temporary physical afflictions induced by traditional healers in Central Africa and anywhere where there is a strong belief in an authority figure having "magical" powers, then responses of this type in situations of high stress, such as fear, are not uncommon. Other forms of physical response may occur, such as loss of speech and even death, as apparently occurred in the similar situation with Ananias and Sapphira. In this story, Elymas, under intense emotional pressure, developed temporary "hysterical" blindness. There is nothing intrinsically impossible or indeed improbable, about this story and it has the features of a well-remembered event that, from Luke's point of view, validated Paul's credentials as an apostle of equal standing with Peter.

The crippled man at Lystra (Acts 14:8–10)

There is no intrinsic impossibility in the view that Paul healed people suffering from the same sort of psychosomatic disorders as those who were healed in the Gospel narratives. In this story there is a considerable amount of development in order to emphasise the theological message that the story embodies, and also to emphasise the fact that Paul undertook exactly the same sort of ministry as that undertaken by Peter. There is thus a significant degree of apologetic design in the way this account is formulated and care should be taken in considering the details given about the actual healing.

The statement that the man had been lame from birth seems to be a clear link with the man at the temple gate at Acts 3:4, and is likely to be part of Luke's emphasis on the hopeless state of the man, and the nature of the mighty act that Paul was about to perform. The language that Luke used is part of good story telling, but this does not negate the probability that Paul undertook the healing of psychosomatic and related conditions as he himself claimed to have preached the gospel with the accompaniment of "signs and wonders" (2 Cor 12:12 and Rom 15:19). It seems likely, therefore, that this story is part of that shift towards more dramatic healings that has already been noted in Luke's writings, and the threefold statement that the man could not use his feet, had been lame from birth, and had never walked may very likely be discounted as a degree of pious exaggeration. It is much more likely that the man was suffering from some form of functional psychogenic lameness, in other words, a conversion disorder, along the lines of those already met in the various Gospel stories. Paul dealt with the situation with the same sort of abreactive technique that has also been met previously.

The girl medium at Philippi (Acts 16:16–18)

This story is of particular interest in that it is the only account of something approaching an exorcism being performed by the apostles. Although Luke referred to both Peter and Paul carrying out such activities (Acts 5:16 and 19:12), it would seem that this is the only example he was able to find in the traditions at his disposal, and it is very different in character from the exorcisms related in the Gospels. Indeed, it hardly seems to be a standard form of exorcism at all. The story involved a slave girl, who was understood to be possessed by the Pythonic god, Apollo, and was employed as a fortune teller. Today she would have been described as a medium. Her case was very different from the people who were classed as "demon possessed" in the Gospel stories, and the girl shows no animosity to Paul and his companions. She simply goes about proclaiming who they were, but in a manner that was making life difficult for all concerned. Paul showed remarkable patience with her, but eventually the nuisance becomes too much and he was forced to deal with her.

The account provides very little detail, but it seems very probable that Paul did no more than unmask a fraudulent medium who may well have been mentally handicapped in some way. That would certainly explain the persistent way she went around following Paul and his colleagues. The method that Paul is said to have used to deal with the girl would seem to be something like the use of an abreactive technique, but this may be no more than the way in which Luke has developed the story and turned the occasion into an exorcism for his own purposes. Paul himself never mentions exorcism in any of his letters nor does he suggest at any time that he may have been involved in the practice. Indeed, he never talked about demons as such, other than to use them as the title of the pagan gods in a disparaging way. It seems very probable, therefore, that Luke has allowed himself some licence in this story. It is a reasonable guess that the original situation may have been no more than Paul telling the girl to go away and stop being a nuisance.

Paul's sweatbands and apron (Acts 19:11-12)

The comments about the extraordinary things that accompanied Paul's ministry closely mirror the remarks about Peter's shadow at an earlier part of the narrative (see above on Acts 5:12-16). Luke is once again emphasising that his hero Paul was of equal spiritual stature to Peter. Thus, just as Peter's shadow somehow was able to pass on divine virtue to those touched by it, so also could Paul's working clothes. It would appear from the narrative that his working aprons and sweat bands (wrapped around his brow to stop the sweat dropping on his work or into his eyes) were being quietly pilfered and used as talismans or charms to cure people of their illnesses. Luke seems to have no problem with the idea that such objects could somehow convey God's healing power, and such ideas gained widespread credence as the cult of saints gathered momentum. Although such ideas may be dismissed as superstition, it should also be recognised that people with various psychosomatic disorders may well have gained some degree of benefit from touching Paul's clothes, in much the same way as sacramental anointing, and saint's relics have provided psychological help, and provided a degree of symptomatic relief in cases of psychosomatic illness over the years. What such actions cannot do is cure genuine organic diseases and change organic pathology.

The possessed man and the sons of Sceva (Acts 19:13-19)

Luke's point in recounting this tale is to emphasise the abject failure of the Jewish exorcists to deal with the possessed man. It is interesting that Paul nowhere comes in touch with this man in the course of the narrative and is not credited with undertaking any exorcism. This would be true to the evidence of Paul's letters which contain no references to exorcism as noted earlier. The man was clearly very violent and the complete failure of the itinerant Jewish exorcists would strongly suggest that he was suffering from a genuine acute organic psychiatric disease, such as paranoid schizophrenia. True psychoses of this nature are not amenable to the abreactive techniques of the traditional healer, any more than they are to various forms of behavioural therapy today. Patients with this type of illness, arising from deep seated disorders of brain chemistry, need to be placed on a strict course of the appropriate modern medications in order to relieve symptoms. It is not surprising that the Jewish exorcists failed so miserably and had to face their patient turning on them in a psychotic rage.

The fall of Eutychus at Troas (Acts 20:7–12)

This little cameo has all the features of an event well-remembered and has a sure ring of authenticity. Paul had met with the Christians at Troas and they were listening to him preach. A young man was there, sitting on the window ledge and, probably tired after a long day at work as well as with the lateness of the hour, and the probable tedium of a long sermon, dozes off (the Greek word is exact, *katapheromenos*). Once he is sound asleep (another exact word, *katenechtheis*) he topples off the window ledge and falls from the third floor to the ground where his friends pick him up, apparently dead. Fortunately, Paul was less precipitate in his judgment and tells the Christians to stop making a fuss for Eutychus was still alive. The young man was unconscious, probably quite severely concussed, and he was possibly put into another room to recover, while Paul shared a meal with his friends, and continued talking until dawn. By this time, Eutychus had made a sufficient recovery for him to be taken home. It is to be hoped that he escaped the long term complications of a closed head injury!

There is nothing that is in any sense "miraculous" in this story, although one gains the impression that Luke would like his readers to see it in that way. However, it does underline the ease with which people were adjudged dead in the ancient world. But for Paul's intervention, it seems quite possible that the poor young man would have been carried off unconscious and quite possibly have been buried alive. It is a story that tends to provide some confirmation of the view that those apparently raised to life by Jesus and the apostles were, in fact, much more likely to have been in a coma or some other unconscious state rather than being clinically dead. This may well have been the case with Ananias and Sapphira (Acts 5:1–11) as already noted.

Paul's eyesight (Acts 23:5)

It was noted, in the discussion of Paul's experience on the Damascus Road and the blindness that followed, that it was highly suggestive of lightning strike injury to the eyes. This form of injury may result in the later development of cataracts as a result of heat damage to the lens. The incident recounted here took place when Paul was before the Jewish Sanhedrin in

Jerusalem. A heated exchange had occurred between Paul and the high priest and when Paul is taken to task about his language, he apologises and says that he did not realise that he was addressing the high priest. This failure to recognise the high priest is suggestive of poor eye sight which might well have been the result of cataract formation following the lightning strike injury, or long term exposure to ultra violet light from the Mediterranean sun, or probably a combination of both. It seems likely that the arrest of Paul in Jerusalem took place around AD 56 or 57 and was thus some twenty years or more after the events on the Damascus Road. This time lapse would have been sufficient to allow for the development of cataracts following the original injury, especially when associated with exposure to high levels of ultra violet light. Cataracts are common among people with long exposures to bright sunshine, such as those who lived in the eastern Mediterranean region.

The degree of visual impairment from cataract formation generally varies according to the density of the cataracts. However, there may be a paradoxical element in that, although distance vision may be markedly impaired, near vision may be unaffected or even improve slightly. The sufferer may thus be able to read and write, but unable to see things clearly at a distance. Assuming that Luke's accounts reflect the reality of Paul's condition, then he would have been able to read, but at the same time would have had problems with distance vision. Thus, when confronted by the high priest, he would have been able to make out a blurred white figure, but unable to distinguish facial features and recognise him. Assuming that this story of Paul's appearance before the Sanhedrin reflects the situation with accuracy (and Paul's failure to recognise the high priest is just the sort of detail that people would remember) then it is certainly consistent with the apostle suffering from cataracts to which his earlier lightning strike injury would have made him more susceptible.

Paul's snakebite (Acts 28:1–6)

Paul and his friends must all have been rather wet and miserable, having scrambled to land on the island of Malta after the shipwreck. Paul was helping to gather sticks for a fire when he was bitten on the hand by a snake that had come out of the firewood due to the warmth of the fire. There are no venomous snakes on the Maltese Islands today, although it is just possible that the common European viper may have been present in

Roman times. It is clear, however, that in this case it was a non-venomous and harmless snake, and Paul suffered no harm from the bite, although the locals believed it was poisonous and expected him to drop down dead. All snakes in the ancient world tended to be viewed as poisonous and little distinction was often made between different species. The local populace changed their minds about Paul's status when he survived the incident and, from thinking he was an escaped murderer, promptly called him a god. There is nothing improbable about the story and T.E. Lawrence (Lawrence of Arabia) describes a similar incident in his own life when a snake came out of the fire having been caught up in the brushwood.

The father of Publius at Malta (Acts 28:8)

It would seem that Paul and his friends were billeted out after the shipwreck and were staying with Publius, "the chief man of the island," a title found in inscriptions and apparently applied to the chief magistrate of the area. His father was ill with dysentery and according to Luke was "gripped" with his symptoms, which included fever and diarrhoea. He would thus appear to have had severe colicky abdominal cramps coupled with profuse bloody diarrhoea. In view of the rapid resolution of symptoms it would seem likely that the illness had arisen from bacterial toxins rather than from actual infection from a food source, such as typhoid, paratyphoid fevers or campylobacter infection. Contamination of food, particularly by flies, is still very common and would have been much more so in the insanitary conditions of the ancient world. The bacteria (frequently *Staphylococcus aureus*) left on the food by the flies rapidly multiply, but are themselves destroyed by cooking. However, the toxins they have produced remain in the food and may produce a short-lived, but severe illness, characterised by fever, abdominal cramps, severe diarrhoea, sometimes with blood, and there is frequently nausea and vomiting. The condition is usually self-limiting and is over in twenty-four hours or so. Another possibility would be an infection from a food-borne virus. These also tend to produce short-lived, but quite severe illnesses that may prostrate the patient. It would seem likely that some such condition accounted for the prostration of Publius' father and Paul's actions may be seen as essentially comforting and reassuring to the patient. The resolution of the illness could hardly be called "miraculous," although that certainly seems to be the impression that Luke wishes to convey.

One thing is certain about this incident: the illness of Publius' father was not Malta fever or brucellosis, although this has been proposed in many commentaries. Brucellosis is an illness characterised by intermittent attacks of low grade fever (hence its other common name, undulant fever), with sweating, loss of appetite, weight loss, aching joints, and general debility. Diarrhoea is not a feature of the illness, and certainly not in the severe form described by Luke. The disease is transmitted most commonly through infected milk or milk products.

It is interesting that Luke continues the narrative by noting that the local population came for treatment (*etherapeuonto*). This is a different verb from the one used for Paul's ministrations and one that would suggest medical treatment rather than an immediate cure. Should Luke, Paul's companion and physician, have been with the party (and this section constitutes one of the famous "we" passages in Acts, suggesting a personal involvement by the author) then the change in verbs suggests that Luke set up practice during their short stay on Malta and charged the local people for his clinical services, thus providing some additional financial support for the party. The value of these services may well account for the remark that Paul and his friends were heaped with gifts before their departure for Rome.

5

The New Testament Letters

IN CONTRAST TO THE Gospels and Acts, the New Testament letters contain remarkably little of medical interest, other than the reference to Paul's "thorn in the flesh." Not only so, but they also present a very different impression from the Gospels and Acts in relation to the cure of disease. In general, the writers of the New Testament letters would appear to take it for granted that diseases will take their natural course without special divine intervention, although they have a high view of the importance and efficacy of prayer.

The Gospels and Acts, although probably written with specific Christian communities in mind, had a general appeal, whereas the New Testament letters were largely written to deal with practical and theological problems that had arisen in the various small Christian communities to which they were addressed. Some of Paul's letters were very obviously "fire-fighting" exercises, written to deal with critical situations with an almost white-hot urgency. The particularity of this material will mean that it is most unlikely to present anything like a complete picture of the wide-ranging and often very diverse beliefs and practices of the early Christian communities. This study is concerned solely with medical matters and, in spite of the specific and local nature of most of the letters, it is one of the more surprising things about this correspondence that there is such a paucity of references to sickness and the healing of disease. It would be reasonable to assume that matters of major importance in the life of the early Church would feature relatively prominently in the letters, but, in spite of the prominence given to healing particularly in the Synoptic Gospels and the book of Acts, there is hardly any mention of the healing of disease and no mention whatsoever of demon possession and exorcism. While prayer for the sick is advocated, the expectation seems to be that the sick will get well by natural processes and not as a result of any special divine intervention. There is a number of occasions when medical terms, such as "gangrene" (2 Tim 2:17), are used figuratively, but as these do not relate to specific medical matters they will not be discussed in this section.

THE PAULINE CORRESPONDENCE

Paul's letters are, in general, the earliest New Testament documents. They were written to churches established during Paul's wide-ranging mission and can be dated roughly between the period spanned by the years AD 48 to 50 and AD 60 to 62, that is beginning within a generation of the first Easter and well before the Gospels. The so-called Pastoral Letters (1–2 Tim and Titus) are generally regarded as not being Pauline compositions, although it is very probable that they contain some genuine Pauline material revamped to meet new circumstances towards the end of the first century. There is also divergence of opinion about whether Ephesians and Colossians are authentically Pauline; probably a majority of scholars opting for the genuiness of Colossians, but not Ephesians.

Paul's understanding of sickness

Jewish religion in New Testament times was greatly influenced by what is called apocalyptic thought. This type of thinking had arisen during periods of calamity and persecution, particularly in the period of the Maccabees and the conflict with imposed Hellenism, when it became a criminal offence to display any hint of Jewishness, and circumcision, the specific mark of being a Jew, was banned. Not surprisingly, apocalyptic thought was marked by a strong feeling of pessimism towards the existing world as well as a strongly particularistic element which not only resisted the influence of Hellenism, but was also strongly anti-heathen and anti-foreign in outlook. The great question was essentially how could the God of Israel allow the persecution of his people for obeying his laws? Punishment for sin was one thing, and was part and parcel of the prophetic message in the Hebrew Bible, but it seemed to the Jews that they were being punished for their obedience to the laws of God. Apocalyptic writers dealt with the problem by consigning the world to the control of evil powers and putting it completely beyond redemption. Only the dramatic intervention of God would change things by bringing a new world into being, and the righteous thus waited in anticipation of the end day, the destruction of the old world, and the bringing in of the new. Ideas of this nature are to be found throughout the New Testament and reflect the Jewish environment out of which it grew. Paul was influenced by such ideas and inevitably they affected his understanding of sickness and health.

Paul viewed disease and death as inevitable corollaries of living in the old world and inevitable facets of human experience, the consequence, in fact, of human sin. Freedom from sickness and death belonged to the future age, the new world that God would eventually bring into being, and could never be achieved in the present age, dominated by evil. The present experience of all humanity is what he called "the bondage of corruption" in which the whole creation shares (Rom 8:19-23). Only the arrival of the future age will bring about the removal of suffering. He used similar language at 1 Cor 15, once again emphasizing the contrast between the present and future states, and using what is essentially dualistic language to speak of the "outward" person being subject to decay and the "inward" being renewed by the presence of Christ through his Spirit.

It is clear that Paul saw sickness (he used the word *astheneia* (weakness) to cover all forms of human weakness, including disease) as part of the normal pattern of human life in the here and now, from which permanent relief will occur only in the future age and the new world yet to be. In passing, it should be noted that nowhere does Paul envisage that the Christian community may have some sort of immunity to disease or that special healing powers will ensure that there will always be immediate and instant cures on demand, an approach to sickness that seems to have become prominent in many Christian circles today.

Finally, it is worth commenting on the only occasion in which Paul appeared to attribute sickness and even death to being the result of specific actions. In the course of a discussion of the way in which the Lord's Supper was being brought into disrepute by the excesses of some in the Corinthian church, he noted that their failure to "discern the body" was bringing judgment upon themselves. To eat and drink "without discerning the body" was to bring judgment upon oneself (1 Cor 11:27-30). This was why many were weak (*astheneis*), ill (*arrōstoi*), and had even died (*koimōntai ikanoi*). It is interesting that nowhere else did Paul suggest that human sickness was the direct result of sin, but in this one passage he regarded sickness and death as a direct judgment on a specific form of behavior that failed to recognize the "body" in the celebration of the Lord's

Supper. What this entailed exactly is a matter for theological debate and is outside the remit of a study concerned primarily with medical issues.

Healing gifts (1 Cor 12:9, 28, 30)

In the light of the current emphasis on healing and healing services in most communions of the Christian Church, it is remarkable that Paul refers to gifts of healing on only one occasion in all his writings, namely at this one section within his first letter to the Corinthians. The idea of such gifts is found nowhere else in the New Testament and it is noteworthy that in other discussions of the gifts and endowments of God's Spirit, such as Rom 12:3–8 and Eph 4:11–16 (although the latter may not be Pauline), there is no reference to healing. It is dangerous to argue from silence, but it would seem very possible that what are referred to as gifts of healing, whatever they may have been, were something unique to the Corinthian church. It appears to have been a disordered and disorderly church that held to an understanding of the kingdom of God as something that was already present in the here and now. The Corinthian Christians appeared to believe that they were living in a world in which the resurrection had already arrived through the presence of the risen Christ among them by his Spirit, thus giving them the power through that Spirit to live on a higher plain than other mortals and, among other things, be able to defeat sickness.

It is impossible to be certain of the meaning of Paul's terminology as the context in which he wrote is largely missing. Someone once remarked that reading Paul's letters is like listening to one half of a telephone conversation. A great deal can be grasped, but a great deal also has to be left to the imagination. Nonetheless, some comment may be made. The word that Paul used to denote healing (*iama*) in this context is an unusual noun derived from a verb that bears the normal meaning of "a means of cure, a medicine, or remedy." In relation to the gifts of healing, the noun occurs in this letter only, and in these three verses only, and nowhere else in the New Testament. The related verb is normally used of physical healing in the New Testament, especially in Luke's Gospel, but it is also used in a more metaphorical manner to speak of restoring or delivering someone from ills of all kinds. At Heb 12:13 and 1 Pet 2:24, for example, the verb is used of spiritual and moral restoration from the effects of sin.

In view of the fact that this noun is found nowhere else in the New Testament, it may be wise not to assume automatically that Paul was referring to the cure of disease, but rather it may be that a special gift was in view that gave some within the community the ability to restore people to what might be called spiritual health. They might have been the sort of people designated "counselors" in modern society. In this regard it is worth making the point that in general, the gifts and endowments that Paul listed all dealt with what may be termed the spiritual needs of the community, with the possible exception of "works of power" (1 Cor 12:10, 29), the exact meaning of which remains unclear. A gift that enabled some to provide physical healing to other members of the congregation seems out of place in a list that related, in all other aspects, to the spiritual welfare and functioning of the community. It is impossible to provide certainty, but one thing is clear: these gifts did not rank high in Paul's thought and he attempted to regulate them in order to avoid the eccentricities and irregularities that marked the behavior of this Corinthian community. There is certainly nothing in Paul's correspondence to suggest that there was any special healing ministry in the communities he or his friends had founded and it is surprising, to say the least, that recent years have seen such an emphasis placed on what appears to have been a side issue in the earliest Christian communities. The mark of the early Church was much more the pastoral care of the sick and others in need and distress, a much more demanding form of ministry.

Paul's health

Paul wrote very little about his health, even in the autobiographical parts of his letters such as 2 Corinthians 11 and 12. The only specific health issue he noted was the "thorn in the flesh" which will be considered separately. However, he did list some of the privations he suffered in the course of his ministry. He recounted episodes of numerous beatings and being at death's door frequently. He spoke of the five times that he took thirty-nine lashes from the Jews, the three occasions when he was beaten with rods, and the time when he was stoned (2 Cor 11:23–25). He went on to describe the cold, the hunger, the sleeplessness, and the toil and hard work that he experienced during his missionary work. There is undoubtedly an element of rhetoric in all this and his lists have frequently been compared with the conventional lists of troubles suffered by moral philosophers in the Roman world. However, when writing to people who knew him well, and knew the nature of his ministry, it would have been foolhardy to have exaggerated merely for the purpose of effect, especially in a context of what appears to have been fairly acrimonious controversy. There can be no doubt that the extensive physical abuse to which the apostle had been subjected over the years would have had a marked effect on his general health. That he survived his beatings and stonings says much for his constitution, but even the strongest will suffer some effects from the type of hardships that Paul described and it is certain that he did not escape unscathed. It is not surprising, therefore, that he wrote of his "thorn in the flesh" within the context of these sufferings.

Paul's "thorn in the flesh" (2 Cor 12:7)

It was once remarked that the list of suggested causes of Paul's "thorn in the flesh" read like the index to a medical textbook. The author has discussed the problem in considerable detail elsewhere,[1] and the discussion here will touch only on the main issues. Inevitably, all the solutions offered to this puzzle must remain speculative, although some are more probable than others. One thing, however, is certain. The "thorn" was a specific physical problem. The various attempts to identify the problem with such things as his persecutions, spiritual temptations, remorse, and so on, all fail to do justice to the text and the context. Paul was, without any reasonable doubt, suffering from some sort of debilitating physical condition which arose at a specific time and, furthermore, in association with a remarkable ecstatic vision. From his description, the condition was in some way humiliating, degrading, inviting invidious comparisons, and perhaps even ridicule.

Paul directly related the onset of the "thorn" to an ecstatic experience which he described at 2 Cor 12:2–10, and which had occurred some fourteen years before the time of writing, thus about AD 40. Although there are major difficulties in dating Paul's life, not least because of the effective impossibility of reconciling Paul's personal reminiscences (Gal 1:11—2:11 and 2 Cor 11:16—12:10) with the very compressed and highly selective account given in Acts, it may be estimated that the ecstatic experience took place sometime between seven and ten years after his conversion and at a time when he was based in or near his home city of

---

1. Howard, *Disease and Healing*, 240–251

Tarsus (Gal 1:12). The experience was clearly one of altered consciousness in which he felt himself to have been transported to a different realm of existence. There are other descriptions in ancient literature of similar states, including the story in the Jewish Talmud of four rabbis who had a similar experience, although in their case the visions were induced by ascetic practices. In Paul's case, he did not know whether he was alive or dead at the time, and his third person descriptions suggest a sense of depersonalization.

Experiences of this type may follow severe injuries, especially head injuries, and constitute what is called the acute organic psychiatric syndrome. They may also be engendered in the laboratory by the electrical stimulation of certain parts of the brain and are closely similar to what have been termed "near death experiences." In this altered state of consciousness patients feel detached and separate from their bodies, feeling as though they are looking down on themselves from a different dimension. The experience is usually remembered as being very pleasant and often associated with great elation. Visual hallucinations are also common. It is dangerous to read back into a different time and different culture modern understandings of brain damaged states, but the neural pathways in the brain have not changed and Paul's description of his experience fits very well with such post-traumatic states of altered consciousness. Paul's extensive early missionary activity (virtually ignored in Acts) was associated with a life of extreme hardship including repeated physical violence (see 2 Cor 11 and 12). No doubt there was an element of rhetorical exaggeration in his descriptions of his life, but there can be no doubt that Paul suffered significant physical abuse in the course of his missionary activities which inevitably must have left its mark on him. The onset of an acute psychiatric organic syndrome would fit well as the aftermath of one of the beatings or the stoning that the apostle mentions. It is immediately after the description of this ecstatic experience that Paul described the onset of his "thorn in the flesh," thus relating it firmly to his previous experience.

It is necessary, in any attempt to understand the nature of Paul's "thorn," to take into account the close temporal relationship between it and his ecstatic experience. Paul makes it clear that he was aware that he now suffered from the "thorn" because of the vision, and it seems clear that he believed the relationship between the two was causal. It has to be accepted that Paul's understanding of causality related to what he understood as the will and purpose of God, but that need not mean that he was mistaken in putting the two things together in a causal relationship. It would seem essential, therefore, to look for a pathology that would account for both the vision and the "thorn."

Many suggestions have been made over the years and include such widely diverse conditions as malaria and severe migraine, but most of them fail to recognize the link between the visionary experience and the onset of the "thorn." It is clear that it was a chronic condition, having lasted fourteen years, yet it was not sufficiently debilitating to prevent his ongoing missionary activities. There are clues in his letter to the Galatians that he was suffering from some form of physical affliction at that time and this may reasonably be linked to the "thorn." The condition was distressing to those who saw him and his general bodily condition was far from impressive (Gal 4:13–15). He felt thoroughly "beaten up" was the way he put it, and was often significantly depressed.

Epilepsy has been a "favorite guess" for many years and it is suggested that Paul may have suffered from the specific condition of post-traumatic epilepsy, that is, epilepsy following directly as a consequence of severe head injury. The vision of heaven would have followed the severe head trauma that would have been an almost inevitable result of a stoning or severe beating, and he was then left with the ongoing complication of post-traumatic epilepsy.

It is estimated that about three per cent of all hospital admissions following head injury are associated with the development of epilepsy. It is thus a relatively common complication and there is no reason to suppose that human responses to injury were any different in the ancient world than they are today. Closed head injuries, associated with local brain damage, are especially liable to the development of this complication, and these are the very sort of injuries that might be expected to follow stoning or beating. The condition usually develops soon after the injury (generally within six months) and is often accompanied by some degree of personality change, especially increased nervousness, irritability, and anxiety. It is of note that Paul seems to have suffered from exactly these features (note for example 1 Cor 2:3). There are also hints in his writings that he may also have suffered from some degree of speech defect that might well have followed significant head trauma. In addition, he makes the very revealing comment at Gal 4:14 that he praised the Galatian Christians for not spitting at him (*oude exeptusate*). The verb used has been described as vulgar Greek, and it is found only here in the New

Testament. Epilepsy was the disease *par excellence* in the ancient world that was always associated with spitting as a defense against its evil influence, something noted by such classical writers as Plautus and Pliny. A diagnosis of post-traumatic epilepsy, probably of a focal (localized) type, would well explain the nature of Paul's "thorn in the flesh," and certainly fits the available evidence. Further, because it is a condition that tends to improve over time, often disappearing altogether, this would also explain the absence of any reference to the condition in his later letters.

"Large letters" (Gal 6:11)

Towards the end of his letter to the Galatian Christians, Paul takes the pen from his secretary and writes some lines in his own handwriting. He began by drawing special attention to what he has written with the words, "See with what large letters I am writing to you with my own hand." These words have been used to add weight to the possibility that Paul suffered from poor eyesight, the argument being that he had to use large letters as he wrote because he would not otherwise have been able to see what he was writing. It is not impossible that this was the case, but it would seem to be more likely that Paul was using the expression as a means of emphasis. Large letters were used in public proclamations and attention was drawn to matters of especial importance by writing in larger letters, particularly at the beginning or end of a document, much as banner headlines are used in newspapers today to emphasize and catch the reader's attention. It is not possible to say conclusively, therefore, whether the "large letters" were or were not the result of Paul's defective eyesight.

Sick people in Paul's letters (Phil 2:25–30, 1 Tim 5:23, 2 Tim 4:20)

It is recognized that the two letters to Timothy and that to Titus were unlikely to have come from the pen of the apostle Paul in their present form. However, these letters almost certainly contain genuine Pauline elements and it is a strong possibility that the traditions about the health of Timothy and Trophimus are genuine.

Epaphroditus (Phil 2:25–30) was the emissary of the Philippian church and had brought some form of assistance to the apostle when in prison. While with Paul he had become very ill and apparently had been close to death. There is no way in which his illness can be identified as no details of any sort are given and any number of conditions could account for such an illness. In the same way no comment can be made about Trophimus (2 Tim 4:20) who was simply left behind ill at Miletus. It is not even known whether he recovered and was able eventually to catch up with the party. It is perhaps pertinent to note, however, that in neither case was there any apparent expectation of some sort of miraculous cure, either at the hands of the apostle or another Christian with some special "gift of healing." Clearly these were genuine physical illnesses and not the sort of psychosomatic problem that would have been amenable to the ministrations of a healer.

The remarks about Timothy's health (1 Tim 5:23), however, are virtually straight out of Hippocratic medical practice. Timothy appears to have suffered from frequent stomach complaints and was drinking nothing but water (the verb *hudropoteō* occurs only here in the New Testament and means to drink water exclusively). It seems very probable that Timothy was suffering from the results of drinking the city water that would have been all too often heavily contaminated. As a result he appears to have developed repeated bouts of gastrointestinal infections. These recurrent episodes, such is the implication of the wording, would be very debilitating and would seriously affect his ministry. Although the true nature of such complaints was not understood, the value of drinking wine rather than water was well known to the ancients. Plutarch in particular recommends wine for stomach ailments as well as a general tonic, something which Paul seems to do here for Timothy.

THE LETTER OF JAMES

This letter in its present form may be a reworking in elegant Greek by a skilful editor of a much earlier document. In its present and final form it may be seen as a product of a wider Hellenistic Judaism, although reflecting an early form of, probably Palestinian, Jewish Christianity, and the tradition that it had come originally from the pen of James the brother of Jesus should not be rejected out of hand. From the medical point of view, the main interest lies in the way those who are described as weak (*asthenei*, usually translated "sick") are to be treated within the community.

"Is any among you weak?" (Jas 5:14–16)

The writer brings together three different types of people who are described as being those "in trouble" (*kakōpathei*), those "in good heart" (*euthumei*), and those who "are weak" (*asthenei*). The last group has almost universally been understood to refer to sick people, as the same word is used for the sick or the weak interchangeably, the context usually making it clear what state is in view. This common interpretation, however, should be questioned, not least because of the very clear link made between this "weakness" and sin. The context as a whole makes it much more likely that the writer is thinking of three mental or emotional states that he sets in contrast. The writer indicates that the person who is in trouble in the sense of having to put up with hardship should pray for strength to be able to endure the burden. Those who are in good heart and cheerful should praise God. The word used for "cheerful" or "in good heart" is rare in the New Testament and occurs elsewhere only in the story of Paul's shipwreck (Acts 27:22 and 25) when Paul exhorts his shipmates to take heart in spite of the imminent disaster.

In contrast with the cheerful group are those who are "weak." However, the weakness seems to be of a very specific sort because the writer refers to them as "weary," "burdened," or "down hearted" (*ta kamnonta*). Their weakness, in fact, is more akin to depression and one, furthermore, that seems to be linked with feelings of guilt. In other words, here was a group of people who were burdened by their consciousness of sin and were becoming depressed as a result. James, in fact, describes them as being weary in their minds, using the verb *kamnō*, used elsewhere in the New Testament of those who were weary and fainthearted (Heb 12:3). In short, they were suffering from that old deadly sin of *accidie*, usually mistranslated as "sloth," but which in reality means a sense of utter despondency and purposelessness in life. The advice given by James is to call for the elders of the congregation and allow them to minister in prayer, and by anointing with oil, which will bring salvation and forgiveness. These are hardly words applicable to normal sickness, but very apt as a way to bring psychological support and help to someone who is weary of life and depressed, particularly should that depression be associated with strong feelings of guilt. People in such a state of mind will benefit greatly from the supportive approach advised by James, and the assurance of forgiveness will be an important factor in assisting their recovery.

Anointing with olive oil (Jas 5:14–15)

Olive oil was widely used throughout the Mediterranean world in food, for ritual and religious purposes, and in medicine. Oil baths and anointing were commonly used, and anointing with oil was especially linked to exorcism (as at Mark 6:13). In the present context the use of olive oil is linked with prayer and the assurance of forgiveness. The act of anointing is thus to reinforce the effect of prayer and provide visible proof of the community's care and support. There is no suggestion that either a medicinal or magical use for the oil is in view in this passage, and it would be completely anachronistic to see it as in some way akin to the practice of sacramental anointing. Indeed, it may be affirmed that this passage provides no support whatever for the practice of anointing the sick in which the action seems to be given some sort of semi-magical healing property. The central emphasis of the passage is, in fact, on prayer, and the anointing is incidental. Prayer would provide the psychological help towards transforming the weak person's mental state and this would be reinforced by the physical act of anointing. The act is not curative, but supportive, providing psychological benefit to someone suffering from guilt-laden depression.

THE BOOK OF REVELATION

The book of Revelation is universally recognized as a difficult book, but the problems of its interpretation are not the concern of this study. It was written to a group of seven Christian communities in Asia Minor, what is now modern Turkey, and contains a considerable amount of interesting local imagery, particularly in the introductory seven letters. One of these passages (Rev 3:18) is of medical interest as it relates to the local medical specialization of treating eye diseases, and there is also a passing comment on herbs as remedies in the closing section of the book (Rev 22:2). In addition, plagues, as evidence of divine judgment, crop up at varying points in the course of the book.

Eye ointment (Rev 3:18)

Laodicea was a prosperous city having an important medical centre that had been established at the time of the Greek geographer, Strabo. It was particularly well-known for its work with eye diseases, and in the mid-first century the famous Greek ophthalmologist Demosthenes Philalethes taught there. He wrote an important treatise on eye diseases that was still consulted into mediaeval times. It seems very probable that the famous "Phrygian powder," used as the base for eye ointments, came from here, as Laodicea was in Phrygia and had one of the most famous eye centers in the region. Galen makes reference to this "Phrygian powder," and in the immediate context also refers to Laodicea on a related matter. It is highly probable that the mention in the book of Revelation to eye ointment (*kollurion*) is an ironic comment on the local pharmaceutical industry. It is very likely that there was a significant commercial enterprise in the manufacture and sale of patent eye ointments which would have been highly lucrative in a world where eye problems were common. Numerous recipes for these eye ointments may be found in the ancient medical texts and they generally included metallic salts such as alum, as well as copper and zinc salts, together with herbal derivatives. The "Phrygian stone" seems very likely to have been alum (aluminium potassium sulphate) which is common in the area as a natural mineral. Its value has long been known as an astringent, and it continues to be used in "styptic pencils" to induce rapid clotting after shaving cuts. However, its use as an eye application would raise some questions today to say the least!

There are many satirical epigrams by the Greek writers about ophthalmologists whose ointments destroyed the sight of those they were supposed to be helping (not altogether surprising if they contained substantial amounts of alum). The same sort of irony is contained in this passage, for the writer is pointing the finger at a community that can claim to be able to deal with the problems of physical eyesight, but has failed dismally to deal with its own spiritual blindness.

Leaves for healing (Rev 22:2)

The final chapters of this book portray a sort of "paradise regained" with the use of images taken from the prophetic books of the Hebrew Bible. One of the pictures, borrowed from the prophet Ezekiel (47:1–12) is of a tree with leaves that were for the "healing of the nations." The use of herbal remedies was one of the standard approaches to medical treatment and the value of astringents such as myrrh, and pain killers such as the opium poppy, were well-known in antiquity. The range of effective drugs, however, was very small and the writer of this book looks to a time when an effective "all heal" would be available to maintain the health of all people. It is of interest that the writer uses the word *therapeia* to emphasise the curative properties of this tree. It is a word that suggests "cure" or possibly even "remedy"—the leaves of this tree possess the remarkable property of being a remedy for all diseases. The imagery is probably as much figurative as anything else, but the passage does draw attention to the limited range of therapeutic agents that were available in the ancient world, and it is also remarkable that this is the only New Testament reference to the use of herbal remedies which were widely known and used in contemporary society.

Plagues (Rev 7:20; 11:6; 15:1, 6, 8; 16:2; etc)

The threat of plagues, that is such a recurring feature of the Book of Revelation, is presented to the reader as a consequence of divine judgment on the world. Plague was a descriptive term for any form of epidemic illness and it is not easy to determine the exact nature of ancient plagues. Ancient documents often refer to such outbreaks of infectious diseases and they tended to arise predominantly in situations of overcrowding and poor hygiene. Indeed, the spread of such infectious diseases is very much a population dependent phenomenon, and the growth of cities in later antiquity was certainly one factor in the occurrence of epidemics. The "plague of Athens" in the fifth century BC was one of the famous examples in ancient history, but there is no general agreement as to its nature. In the Hebrew Bible there is a reference to a plague affecting the Philistines that was very likely genuine bubonic plague (1 Sam 5:6–12) in view of the references to both the swollen lymph nodes in groin and arm pits (often called "buboes" and hence the name bubonic plague), and "mice" associated with the disease. Rats and mice were not distinguished in Hebrew, but a major infestation of rodents had occurred and was destroying the crops and it is possible that these rodents were rats whose fleas were carrying bubonic plague with them into local dwellings. Other common causes of such outbreaks would have been smallpox and typhoid fever, but the great majority of references to such outbreaks in the ancient literature are too vague for certainty about the cause.

The language in Revelation is largely figurative, but the references to pain, "foul and evil sores," and possibly burning sensations (Rev 16:2, 8–11) would certainly fit with a description of bubonic plague as the supreme example of a disastrous epidemic, although smallpox could also fit the description. It is not surprising that such dreadful visitations were considered to be a judgment poured out by God. However, although the identification of John's plagues with bubonic plague seems possible, any real diagnosis is precluded by the vagueness of the descriptions and the symbolic context of the writing. Furthermore, as noted earlier, any epidemic disease with a high mortality would be labeled a "plague."

Plague itself, however, which is the disease caused by infection with the bacterium *Pasteurella pestis,* was a form of epidemic disease that was widely known in the ancient world and its unpleasant effects, and high mortality would always make it a suitable vehicle for a divine judgment. The great plagues that affected Europe in the time of Justinian (sixth century) and in the mediaeval and later periods (such as the Black Death and the Great Plague of London) were similarly seen as divine visitations on a sinful community, rather than as the inevitable result of overcrowding, poor hygiene, and no efficient control of vermin. Whether these plagues, however, were all examples of bubonic plague, as has generally been considered, is a view that has been questioned in recent years, and the Black Death in particular has been judged by some authors to have been a form of viral disease of great virulence (such as some form of one of the viral hemorrhagic fevers). As far as the author of Revelation was concerned, diagnosis in the modern sense was unknown and any major epidemic would have been seen as a judgment of God upon a sinful humanity, an outlook which has not entirely disappeared even in the twenty-first century.

6

Medical Metaphors and Allusions in the New Testament

IT IS NOT SURPRISING to find a range of medical terms used in reports of general speech and in written communications in the New Testament. Such metaphors and allusions were common in general writings of the time as they are today. They provide a window into many of the general ideas of the time about human anatomy as well as the nature of disease, quite apart from the literary or theological interest of the use of the allusions themselves.

WORDS FOR SICKNESS AND DISEASE

The normal Greek word for disease or illness is *nosos*, but it is a word very rarely used in the New Testament, occurring on just eleven occasions in the Gospels and Acts. It is not used in a metaphorical manner in the New Testament, although some of the early Church Fathers used the word in this way to speak of human vice. The related verb, "to be sick" (*nosein*), on the other hand is never used literally of illness at all. It does occur once only in a figurative sense at 1 Tim 6:4. Here it describes the "sickness" of mind of the person who persists in argument, disputation, and perverse speculation. The word most commonly used for sickness, whether actual or metaphorical, is *astheneia*, a word having the literal meaning of "weakness." The related verb (*asthenein*) and adjective (*asthenēs*) are also commonly used. In the Gospels this word family is almost always used literally, but in the New Testament letters the meaning is often figurative, and at times it is not always easy to draw the line between metaphorical and literal usages. The word always retains its basic meaning of being weak, either literally in the sense of being weak as a result of illness, or weak as opposed to being strong physically, and also weak in a figurative sense.

Paul can thus speak, for example, of those who are "weak in faith" (Rom 14:1–2), and who become over-scrupulous in their religious observances (as also at 1 Cor 8:11–12). In a similar vein, the law is "weak" because it has no power to overcome human failure and can only point to the right way to behave (Rom 8:3). A similar word for weakness (*arrhōstos*) is occasionally used of sickness in the Gospels and once at 1 Cor 11:30 in conjunction with *asthenēs* to describe the physical state ("weak and sickly") of those who fail to treat the Lord's Supper in an appropriate manner. It is not used in a metaphorical sense of moral weakness.

In addition, there is a number of other words used to describe illness and its effects, but these are used in a literal manner of genuine sickness, rather than being used metaphorically of moral states that may be compared to genuine disease.

WORDS ABOUT MEDICAL TREATMENT, CURE, AND HEALTH

The Greek goddess of health was named Hygeia from which the English word "hygiene" is derived. Things that are hygienic are considered to be conducive to good health, and the improvements in hygiene conditions, with better water supplies and sanitation, have resulted in improved levels of health in the community. However, the Greek noun for "health" (*hugieia*) is not found in the New Testament, although the adjective "healthy" (*hugiēs*) and the verb "to be healthy" (*hugiainō*) are found on twelve occasions each, often in a figurative sense. It is worth noting that health as a concept does not figure highly in either the Hebrew Bible or the New Testament, and it is the figurative and metaphorical use of this word group that predominates. The verb is used very sparingly of physical health and, apart from Luke, is found elsewhere in this sense only in the story of the healing of the man at the Pool of Bethesda in John 5. Jesus used the verbal form in the proverbial saying, "they that are healthy do not need the physician, but those who are sick" (Luke 5:31), and in that particular context the word was referring to the tax collectors and the other less than socially desirable characters with whom Jesus mixed, and whom he called to repentance and a better life.

The verb is also used in the Pastoral Letters (1 and 2 Timothy and Titus) in a figurative way and these letters include most of the occasions on which the verb occurs in the New Testament (1 Tim 1:10; 6:3; 2 Tim

1:13; 4:3 and Tit 1:9, 13; 2:1, 2). The writer uses the verb to describe wholesome teaching and a healthy faith as opposed to that which is unhealthy or false. This sort of metaphorical use is to be found in many of the Greek writers as well as in the works of Josephus. As a metaphor it may convey the idea of being safe and sound, or may simply refer to that which is wholesome or fitting. In the Septuagint version of the Hebrew Bible, the verb generally translates the Hebrew word *šalôm* usually translated as "peace," but which has a much wider meaning than the word generally conveys in English, including an individual's total well-being or health in physical, mental, and spiritual terms.

The English word "therapy," to describe a form of medical treatment, derives from the Greek verb *therapeuō*, a verb that had a wide range of meaning. Originally it meant to be an attendant, or to serve or be serviceable, and the related noun (*therapeia*) referred to the service given. It was used in this way at Luke 12:42 of the diligent servant who maintained his master's household in the proper way. It was also used of service to the gods. The word group always carried the idea of willing service and of solicitude for the one in need. It was the ideal word to describe the work of the physician or surgeon in providing a service for the sick person at a time of need, and it thus came to have the meaning of providing medical treatment. In the New Testament it is this medical use of the word that dominates. The verb is used on forty-three occasions, and is almost entirely limited to Matthew and Luke/Acts where it should in many cases be translated "treat" rather than "heal." There is no doubt that at Acts 28:9 the verb means to treat (referring to the medical services of Luke) in contrast to the healing (using a different verb) undertaken by Paul. It is thus not used in a figurative or metaphorical sense, but in the exact way that describes a form of service, whether medical or in more general terms.

The other word group commonly used for healing and cure (verb *iaomai*, nouns *iasis*, and rarely *iama*) is the one from which the standard word for a physician in Greek is derived (*iatros*). Once again it is a word particularly favored by Luke. These words are rarely used in a figurative sense and almost entirely relate to physical healing other than in six cases. In three of these (Matt 13:15; John 12:40; Acts 28:27) the verb comes in a quotation of Isaiah 6:10 where the rebellion of the people against their God is compared with physical disability that requires to be healed or cured. The remaining three occasions in which the verb is used in this metaphorical sense occur at Heb 12:13, Jas 5:16, and 1 Pet 2:24. In each case the underlying concepts are very similar, the word being used to speak of healing the damaged spirits of the weaker members of the community.

The final verb to be considered and used in a context of healing and cure is the verb "to save" (*sōzō*). The primary meaning is, as in English, to deliver or snatch a person from grave and immediate peril. As in English, however, so also in Greek, and the word came to take on a wider range of meaning in general and religious terms. In particular, the word took on ideas of bringing benefit, of keeping and preserving, and it is in this sense that it is used in relation to the cure of illness. The idea of escape and rescue has virtually vanished and instead there is a sense, not merely of cure, but also of ongoing well-being and good health. The person who has been "saved" in this sense has been restored to functional integrity, not simply cured of a disease. It is this sense of restoration that underlies its use in the healing stories in the Gospels.

The predominant usage of the verb in the New Testament, however, is metaphorical in relation to religious concepts, primarily concerning the restoration of relationships between God and his people. Its use in regard to the cure of disease is restricted, although at Mark 5:34 and 10:52 (and parallels) Jesus uses the important phrase, "your faith has saved/cured you." There seems little doubt that the evangelist was being deliberately ambiguous in his use of words in the story of the woman with the hemorrhage in Mark 5:34. The sick woman's faith removed the "torment" of her condition so that she may now "go in peace," for not only has she been cured (*hugiēs*) of her chronic illness, but more importantly she has been "saved" (*sesōken*), thus restoring her to proper relationships within the community. In this way the stories of healings in the Gospels become parables of the good news, and the deliverance from a disease was used as a symbol of the comprehensive deliverance of the whole person from the bondage of sin and death. It is not surprising that the therapeutic model became a popular image in the early church as it expanded into the Roman world in which the ideas of salvation and saviors was well established. Nonetheless, the use of the verb is relatively infrequent outside the Gospels and Acts where it is used sixty-four times against thirty-seven times in the New Testament letters. The noun is used even less frequently, no doubt because of its strong pagan background.

WORDS ABOUT HUMAN ANATOMY

Knowledge of human anatomy was extremely limited in New Testament times. There was a good understanding of bony structure and muscles arising from the frequent trauma that marked everyday life as well as the result of war wounds, and there are references to bones and ligaments in the New Testament, occasionally in a metaphorical sense (as for example at Col 2:19). However, knowledge of internal organs was vague to say the least, and the functions were only poorly understood. The word *koilia* for example, came from a root that meant a hollow or cavity and was used of the whole body cavity, including the chest cavity as well as the abdomen. This seems to be the meaning at John 7:38 for example. The word could have more specific meanings, however, such as the intestines (1 Cor 6:13) or the uterus (or womb) and it is, in fact, the normal word for the uterus in the New Testament rather than the more usual Greek words, *hustera* (Matt 15:17; 19:12; Luke 1:15, 41, 42; 11:27; Gal 1:15, etc) or *mētra* (used on only two occasions in the New Testament at Luke 2:23 and Rom 4:19). On the other hand, the word might also be used in a figurative sense, and Paul used it in this way to describe the baser human appetites (Rom 16:17; Phil 3:19). The word for stomach (*gastēr*) was not an accurate term and really meant the paunch, referring to an obese abdomen, as well as everything contained in it. It was thus frequently used of the uterus, because of the swollen abdomen of a pregnant woman, and it is used in this way in the birth narratives of both Matthew and Luke (Matt 1:18, 23 and Luke 1:31), as well as in the descriptions of the apocalyptic woes of the last times (Matt 24:19; Mark 13:17; Luke 21:23; 1 Thess 5:3, and note Rev 12:2). In fact, the word is never used of the stomach itself other than in a figurative sense for gluttony and greed in just one instance at Tit 1:12.

Emotions tended to be ascribed in a general way to all the internal organs (*splanchna*). This was again a word with a wide range of meaning and was used to include particularly those internal organs known as the "nobler viscera," that is the heart, lungs, liver, and kidneys. It is used in its literal sense on only one occasion in the New Testament, on the occasion of the death of Judas Iscariot when his abdomen was ruptured and his internal organs (presumably in this case, his intestines) fell out (Acts 1:18). However, the various sensations that seemed to be experienced in the internal organs as a result of emotional feelings understandably led to the belief that emotions arose in these organs, rather than being the result of brain and related neural activity. Indeed, the function of the brain was not understood in any way in ancient times. The word for the various internal organs of the body is thus used frequently to speak of the deeper and kindly emotions of affection, sympathy, and compassion (2 Cor 6:12; 7:15; Phil 1:8; 2:1, etc). The related verb occurs solely in the Gospels to speak of a level of pity that moves people to the depths of their beings, and especially of Jesus showing compassion for the leaderless crowds. He was described as "being moved with compassion," an expression that well described the internal sensations associated with great emotion.

It was the heart (*kardia*), however, that was understood to be the real centre of life and the seat of emotions (especially love), of volition, of thought, of moral decision making, and generally, in fact, as the centre of all physical, spiritual, and mental life. Its proper function in the body, as the pump for blood circulation, was not understood and because of the marked variations in heart rate with changing emotions, it was not surprising that it came to be seen as the centre of such emotions. This understanding was not confined to the Greek world, but was general throughout the ancient world, and such usage has persisted into common English parlance to the present day. The biblical, and particularly the New Testament, references are far too numerous to record, but can be found with the help of any good concordance. There was no knowledge of either the circulation or the functions of the blood, but it was recognized that blood was somehow essential for life and blood loss, if uncontrolled, would result in death. The Jewish people consequently understood blood to be in some way the life principle, and used expressions such as "the life is in the blood" and to kill was to "shed blood." Blood was also used in conjunction with the word flesh to indicate the substance of the human body.

The word flesh (*sarx*) had a wide range of meaning in the New Testament. It could mean the constituents of the human body, especially of the muscle mass that clothed the skeleton, as opposed to the internal organs. In this sense it was used to refer to the totality of a living person (Luke 24:39; 1 Cor 15:39; Gal 2:20), particularly when linked with blood (1 Cor 15:50; Eph 6:12; Heb 2:14) and the expression "flesh and blood" is still used in common speech. In a general sense the word spoke of all human beings and could be translated "humanity" (Rom 3:20). The description of human beings in this way is an essential element of biblical anthropology. People are to be understood primarily in respect of their relation to God. As a creature, created by God, a person is flesh and subject to death. Human beings (and animals too for that matter) have life because the breath (spirit) of God makes them living beings. The word was also widely used in Greek literature in a figurative sense as the general seat of affections and desires, and of the physical aspect of life as opposed to the spiritual. Such usage is also to be found in the New Testament where it also becomes the expression of the baser aspects of human character (Rom 7:18; 8:5, 8, 9; 2 Cor 7:1; Gal 5:16, 19; Eph 2:3, etc). In this sense, as descriptive of humanity's wrong dispositions, it should be clearly distinguished from the word *sōma* which simply meant the whole mortal body, whether alive or a dead corpse. The word was sometimes used, however, to mean the vehicle of normal physical life which was seen as separate from the soul or spirit (1 Cor 5:3; 1 Thess 5:23), but its distinctive metaphorical use is specific to the Pauline letters where the local Christian community is spoken of as the "body of Christ" (1 Cor 12:12, 13, 27, etc) and the whole Christian church is given this title at Eph 1:23 and Col 1:18.

Various other parts of the body, such as the hands, head, the loins, and kidneys are given figurative meanings in several places in the New Testament in much the same way as some of them still are in common English usage. These references do not require further remark other than to note that the liver is not mentioned anywhere in the New Testament, although there are several references to it in the Hebrew Bible. Those references do not suggest that it was considered to be the seat of the soul which was a view espoused by some early Jewish writers.

WORDS ABOUT PATHOLOGICAL STATES

There are few medical terms used in the New Testament in a metaphorical way, other than those in general use, such as blindness for lack of spiritual insight (Rom 2:9; 2 Pet 1:9; Rev 3:17). An unusual word to describe dullness of spiritual perception occurs at Mark 3:5; Rom 11:25 and Eph 4:18. This word (*pōrōsis*) basically means a kind of stone similar to marble, and by extension it was used in a medical sense of callus formation in a broken bone, and of bladder stones. The basic meaning is thus of something as hard and unyielding as bone or marble, and it is not difficult to see how it came to be used figuratively of obtuseness of perception or insensitivity to another's need. In the biblical texts it is often associated with the heart and it is then usually translated as "hardness of heart," a situation in which a person is impervious to any form of moral direction or guidance. The related verb occurs on five occasions to describe the same situation.

There are two other words of medical interest. The first is gangrene (*gangraina*) which occurs at 2 Tim 2:17 to describe the dire effects of what the writer calls "godless chatter" that eats its way into a person's spiritual life and effectively kills it. Gangrene itself is the death of tissue as a result of poor or absent blood supply and often may be associated with infection or as the result of conditions such as diabetes and arteriosclerosis. The word occurs in the writings of Hippocrates and Galen to describe gangrene of a limb, particularly arising after injury such as a fracture. It was nearly always fatal, and thus the writer's use of the term makes for a vivid metaphor. Once a limb becomes gangrenous, amputation may often be the only way to stop the gangrene from spreading. One commentator has remarked, "The spread and deadly result of false teaching could not be more aptly described."

The other word of interest is used by Paul in relation to his experience of the risen Christ. At 1 Cor 15:8 he writes that last of all Christ had appeared to him as "one untimely born," as most English versions have it. The Greek word *ektrōma* means an abortion or miscarriage, and it was used as a term of contempt of someone beneath any consideration. Paul's enemies at Corinth appeared to have used this term about him and now he is turning it back on them. They may see him as "Paul, the abortion," but it is to this one that the risen Christ appeared personally. The false teachers at Corinth could never make that claim with any conviction.

Glossary

Abreaction: A form of treatment of certain mental states that causes the patient to work through suppressed emotions.

Ankylosing spondylitis: A chronic spinal disease that produces a progressive arthritis with increasing stiffness of the spine, so that eventually the back becomes completely immobile and often bent.

Bipolar disorder: A major mental illness characterized by cyclical swings of mood between major depression and manic behavior.

Catatonia: A state in which the patient is completely immobile and appears to be in a coma. The patient is unresponsive to stimuli and shows no voluntary movements. It arises in certain forms of mental illness.

Conversion disorders: A term used to describe mental illnesses in which the patient displays the symptoms and signs of physical illness, such as paralysis, blindness, deafness, and loss of sensation in various parts of the body, in order to escape from some form of unpleasant or demanding situation, which may not always be recognized by the patient. No underlying physical cause for the symptoms exists and the features are the result of the "conversion" of emotional stress into physical symptoms. *Abreactive* methods have been used to treat these conditions in the past.

Cataract: The progressive loss of translucency in the lens of the eye so that vision is increasingly restricted, and total blindness may eventually develop. It is particularly common in countries where there are high levels of ultra violet light from constant sunshine.

Chromosome: Structures existing within the nucleus of the cells of living organisms that carry the genetic material in the form of special proteins called genes. Normal human cells carry forty-six chromosomes, but sperm and ova carry half that number allowing for recombination in matched pairs to the normal number following fertilization. The male, however, always has one unmatched pair (X and Y) that determines sex, whereas the female always carries a corresponding matched pair (X and X). Recombination allows for the increase of genetic diversity within the species.

Couching: An ancient method of treating cataracts by either pressing on the front of the eye (manual couching) or by passing a needle through the eye to cause the lens to fall back into the chamber of the eye. This allows light to pass through the eye once again, although there is usually some blurring of vision caused by the loss of focusing through the absence of the lens. The great composer George Frederick Handel was treated in this way, but without success. The method is still used by folk healers in many parts of the world.

Dissociative illness: This used to be called "hysterical neurosis," and is the underlying condition responsible for conversion reactions.

Dystonia: The term refers to abnormally increased muscle tone leading to fixed and abnormal postures. The muscle spasm may be permanent. Focal dystonia occurs in a localized situation in the body, and includes such conditions as "writer's cramp."

Edema: An excess of fluid in the tissues of the body, most often seen in the dependent parts of the body such as the feet and legs. Ascites is the name given to excess fluid in the body cavity. The accumulation of fluid may be localized or generalized throughout the body. There are many causes, but it is usually as a result of failure of the heart, kidneys, or liver.

Hypovolemic shock: Shock arising from the loss of body fluids, usually from excessive bleeding (hemorrhage) or extreme dehydration. Without rapid replacement of body fluids it may be fatal.

Kyphosis: A forwards curvature of the spine (see also scoliosis).

Menorrhagia: Excessive bleeding at the time of a menstrual period. It may be the result of pathology in the uterus, such as tumors (most often not malignant), or hormonal upsets. It should be distinguished from metrorrhagia which describes bleeding between periods.

Metabolic: Relating to the whole range of biochemical reactions that occur in the body to maintain life. Metabolic diseases are those diseases that cause upsets of these processes, such as diabetes and thyroid diseases, as well as the many genetic conditions that may affect specific processes.

Osteomyelitis: Infection of bone, almost always becoming a chronic condition before the advent of antibiotics.

Osteoporosis: Thinning of the bone substance, making bones more prone to fracture. It is common in old age and often linked with low calcium intake in the diet.

Pathology: The study of disease processes and the disease processes themselves. Disease thus produces pathological changes in healthy tissue.

Protozoal: Relating to protozoa, single celled organisms, such as ameba. Most are harmless, but some may be responsible for diseases in humans and animals, such as malaria, relapsing fever, amebic dysentery, and sleeping sickness.

Psoriasis: A common skin condition characterized by patches of reddened plaques in the skin, often covered by what look like silvery scales. The condition may be very extensive, and at times disabling, and disfiguring.

Psychosomatic/psychogenic conditions: Illnesses in which physical symptoms are mainly or entirely the result of psychological factors.

Schizophrenia: A serious mental illness in which the patient usually shows a variety of bizarre and inappropriate forms of behavior. Among the manifestations of the illness are bizarre delusions, especially of a grandiose and persecutory nature, and hallucinations, often in the form of voices speaking to the patient. The patient may be violent and invariably shows some degree of impairment of personal care and hygiene, together with peculiarities of speech. The disease appears to have a strong genetic component that causes the disturbances to brain chemistry which in turn result in the manifestations of the disease.

Scoliosis: A lateral (sideways) curvature of the spine in contrast to a forward curvature (kyphosis, which see).

Seborrheic dermatitis: A very common skin condition, mainly affecting the scalp and face, but which may also occur over the body. The eruption appears as greasy, scaling patches. Dandruff is one of the commonest presentations of this condition and is often associated with the action of skin fungi.

Sympathetic nervous system: Part of the nervous system that operates below the conscious level and affects blood vessels, the muscles of internal organs, and the various glands of the body. It is involved in regulating such functions as blood pressure, and is part of the complex system that regulates the internal environment of the body.

Bibliography

THE BIBLIOGRAPHY THAT FOLLOWS includes those works referred to in the footnotes as well as a selection of relatively recent titles that deal with medical practice in the period of the New Testament and/or the healing practices of the early Christian community. The volumes listed combine both specifically medical as well as more theological studies. Few journal articles have been listed as the general reader is likely to have difficulties tracking down specialized journals. Most of the books mentioned contain their own extensive bibliographies to direct those wishing to delve further into the subject to a wider range of literature. The presence of a volume in this list does not necessarily indicate the present writer's agreement with its contents.

Amundsen, D. W. *Medicine, Society and Faith in the Ancient and Mediaeval Worlds.* Baltimore, MD: Johns Hopkins University Press, 1996.
Brown, R. E. *The Birth of the Messiah: A Commentary on the Infancy Narratives in Matthew and Luke.* New York: Image, 1979.
Browne, S. G. *Leprosy in the Bible.* 3rd edition. London: Christian Medical Fellowship, 1979.
Capps, Donald. *Jesus the Village Psychiatrist.* Louisville, KY: Westminster John Knox, 2008.
Cochrane, R. G. *Biblical Leprosy: A Suggested Interpretation.* London: Tyndale Press, 1961.
Conrad, L. I., et al. *The Western Medical Tradition: 800 BC to AD 1800.* Cambridge: Cambridge University Press, 1995.
Daunton-Fear, Andrew. *Healing in the Early Church: The Church's Ministry of Healing and Exorcism from the First to the Fifth Century.* Milton Keynes: Paternoster, 2009.
Dawson, Audrey. *Healing, Weakness and Power: Perspectives on Healing in the Writings of Mark, Luke and Paul.* Milton Keynes: Paternoster, 2008.
Dunn, J. D. G. *A New Perspective on Jesus: What the Quest for the Historical Jesus Missed.* London: SPCK, 2005.
Edelstein, L. *Ancient Medicine.* Baltimore, MD: Johns Hopkins University Press, 1987.
Faraone, C. A., and D. Obbink, editors. *Magika Hiera: Ancient Greek Magic and Medicine.* Oxford: Oxford University Press, 1991.
Ferngren, G. B. *Medicine and Health Care in Early Christianity.* Baltimore MD: Johns Hopkins University Press, 2009.

Greenwood, W. A. "Leprosy." *The Bible Educator* 4 (1876) 76–78.
Grmek, M. D. *Diseases in the Ancient Greek World*. Baltimore, MD: Johns Hopkins University Press, 1989.
Hobart, W. K. *The Medical Language of St Luke*. Dublin: Dublin University Press, 1892
Howard, J. Keir. *Disease and Healing in the New Testament: An Analysis and Interpretation*. Lanham, MD/Oxford: University Press of America, 2001.
Jackson, R. P. J. *Doctors and Diseases in the Roman Empire*. London: British Museum, 1988.
Kee, H. C. *Medicine, Miracle and Magic in New Testament Times*. Cambridge: Cambridge University Press, 1986.
King, H. *Health in Antiquity*. London: Routledge, 2005.
Kiple, K. F., editor. *The Cambridge World History of Human Diseases*. Cambridge: Cambridge University Press, 1993.
Lloyd Davies, T. A., and Margaret Lloyd Davies. "Resurrection or resuscitation?" *Journal of the Royal College of Physicians London* 25 (1991) 167–170.
Lloyd-Davies, M., and T. A. Lloyd-Davies. *The Bible: Medicine and Myth*. 2nd edition. Cambridge: Silent Books, 1993.
Maslen, Matthew, and Piers Mitchell. "Medical theories on the cause of death in crucifixion." *Journal of the Royal Society of Medicine* 99 (2006) 185–188.
Micklem, E. R. *Miracles and the New Psychology*. Oxford: Oxford University Press, 1922
Nutton, Vivian. *Ancient Medicine*. London: Routledge, 2004.
Palmer, B., editor. *Medicine in the Bible*. Exeter: Paternoster, 1986.
Pilch, J. *Healing in the New Testament: Insights from Medical and Mediterranean Anthropology*. Philadelphia: Fortress, 2000.
Pilowsky, I. *Abnormal Illness Behaviour*. Chichester: Wiley, 1997.
Rosner, F. *Encyclopedia of Medicine in the Bible and Talmud*. New York: Aronson, 2000.
Sargant, William. *Battle for the Mind: The Physiology of Conversion and Brainwashing*. London: Heinemann, 1957
———. *The Mind Possessed*. London: Heinemann, 1973.
Scarborough, J. *Roman Medicine*. London: Thames and Hudson, 1969.
Temkin, O. *Hippocrates in a World of Pagans and Christians*. Baltimore, MD: Johns Hopkins University Press, 1991.
Weatherhead, L. *Psychology, Religion and Healing*. London: Hodder, 1951.
Wilkinson, J. *The Bible and Healing: A Medical and Theological Commentary*. Edinburgh: Handsel Press, 2000.

Scripture Index

OLD TESTAMENT

Genesis

18	50

Exodus

4:6	20
4:11	32
12:46	42

Leviticus

13	20
14	20
15:25–27	27
26:16	10

Numbers

9:12	42

Deuteronomy

28:27	11

1 Samuel

1	50
5:6–12	101

2 Samuel

4:4	23
23:10	25

1 Kings

17:17–24	55

2 Kings

4:18–37	55

Psalms

69:22	40
121:6	35

Isaiah

6:10	105
7:14	52
35:6	32
56:10	32

Ezekiel

47:1–12	100

Joel

2:28	73

NEW TESTAMENT

Matthew

1:18–25	51
1:18	107
1:23	107
4:23–25	44
4:24	35
8:1–4	19
8:5–13	15, 62
8:14–15	18
8:28–34	25
9:1–8	22
9:18–19	29
9:20–22	27
9:23–26	29
9:27–34	47
9:27–31	46
9:32–33	46
12:9–14	24
12:22–23	47
12:24	46
12:27	70
13:15	105
15:17	107
15:21–28	30
16:17	70
17:14–20	35
17:15	35
19:12	107
20:29–34	37, 46
24:19	107
27:5	72
27:26–50	37
27:32	38
27:34	39
27:48	39

Mark

1:11	53
1:21–28	16
1:29–31	18
1:30–31	62
1:40–45	19, 60
2:1–12	22, 64
3:1–6	24
3:5	109
3:22–40	46
3:22	8
5:1–20	25
5:21–24	29
5:25–34	27
5:34	106
5:35–43	29
6:13	99
7:24–30	30
7:31–37	32
8:22–26	33, 65, 66
8:23	32
9:14–29	35
9:18	24
9:38	70
10:46–53	37
10:52	106
13:17	107
15:15–38	37
15:21	38
15:23	39
15:36	39

Luke

1:7	49
1:13	49
1:15	107
1:18–23	48
1:18	49
1:26–38	51
1:31	107
1:41–42	107
1:57–58	49
1:59–65	48
1:62	49

2:23	107	8:41	51
3:16	73	9:1–41	64
4:31–37	16	9:2	65
4:38–39	18	9:6	32
5:12–16	19	11:1–44	66, 80
5:21–32	22	12:40	105
5:31	104	19:1–37	37
6:6–11	24	19:29–30	39
7:1–10	15, 62	19:31–33	42
7:11–17	55, 80	19:17	38
8:26–39	25	19:23	38
8:41–42	29	19:34	40
8:43–48	27	20:27	39
8:49–56	29		
9:37–43	35	**Acts**	
10:29–37	57		
11:15	46	1:18–19	72, 107
11:24–26	17	2:1–4	72
11:27	107	3:1–10	75
12:13–14	21	3:2	65
12:42	105	3:4	81
13:10–17	57	5:1–11	76, 84
14:1–6	2, 59	5:12–16	77, 83
17:11–19	60	5:16	82
18:35–43	37	9:1–19	77
21:23	107	9:33–35	79
22:43–44	40	9:36–43	79
22:49–51	60	10:9–16	74
23:24–46	37	10:15	21
23:26	38	12:20–23	80
23:36	39	13:6–12	76, 80
24:39–40	39	14:8–10	81
24:39	108	14:8	65
		16:9–10	74
John		16:16–18	82
		19:11–12	83
1:45	51	19:12	82
4:46–54	15, 62	19:13–19	83
5	104	20:7–12	77, 84
5:1–18	63	22:3–16	77
6:42	51		
7:38	107		
8:19	51		

Acts (continued)

23:5	84
26:9–19	77
26:13	78
27:22	98
27:25	98
28:1–6	85
28:8	86
28:9	105
28:27	105

Romans

1:3–4	53
2:9	109
3:20	108
4:19	107
7:18	109
8:3	104
8:5–9	109
8:19–23	90
11:25	109
12:3–8	91
14:1–2	104
15:19	81
16:17	107

1 Corinthians

2:3	95
5:3	109
6:13	107
8:11–12	104
11:27–30	90
11:30	104
12	73
12:9	91
12:10	92
12:12	109
12:13	109
12:27	109
12:28	91
12:29	92
12:30	91
15	90
15:8	110
15:39	108
15:50	108

2 Corinthians

6:12	108
7:1	109
7:15	108
11	94
11:16–12:10	93
11:23–25	92
12	94
12:2–10	93
12:7	93
12:12	81

Galatians

1:11–2:11	93
1:12	94
1:15	107
2:20	108
4:13–15	95
4:14	95
5:16	109
5:19	109
6:11	96

Ephesians

1:23	109
2:3	109
4:11–16	91
4:18	109
6:12	108

Philippians

1:8	108
2:1	108

2:25–30	96
3:19	107

Colossians

1:18	109
2:19	107
4:14	7

1 Thessalonians

5:3	107
5:23	109

1 Timothy

1:10	104
5:23	96, 97
6:3	104
6:4	103

2 Timothy

1:13	104
2:17	89, 110
4:3	105
4:20	96, 97

Titus

1:9	105
1:12	107
1:13	105
2:1–2	105

Hebrews

2:14	108
12:3	98
12:13	91, 105

James

5:14–16	97, 99
5:16	105

1 Peter

2:24	91, 105

2 Peter

1:9	109

Revelation

3:17	109
3:18	99
7:20	101
11:6	101
12:2	107
15:1	101
15:6	101
15:8	101
16:2	101
16:8–11	101
22:2	99, 100

www.ingramcontent.com/pod-product-compliance
Lightning Source LLC
Chambersburg PA
CBHW070922160426
43193CB00011B/1557